teach

yourself

quick fix
html

teach yourself®

quick fix
html
mac bride

For over 60 years, more than 40 million people have learnt over 750 subjects the **teach yourself** way, with impressive results.

be where you want to be with **teach yourself**

For UK orders: please contact Bookpoint Ltd., 130 Milton Park, Abingdon, Oxon OX14 4SB. Telephone: +44 (0)1235 827720. Fax: +44 (0)1235 400454. Lines are open 09.00–18.00, Monday to Saturday, with a 24-hour message answering service. You can also order through our website www.teachyourself.co.uk

For USA order enquiries: please contact McGraw-Hill Customer Services, PO Box 545, Blacklick, OH 43004-0545, USA. Telephone: 1-800-722-4726. Fax: 1-614-755-5645.

For Canada order enquiries: please contact McGraw-Hill Ryerson Ltd., 300 Water St, Whitby, Ontario L1N 9B6, Canada. Telephone: 905 430 5000. Fax: 905 430 5020.

Long renowned as the authoritative source for self-guided learning – with more than 40 million copies sold worldwide – the *Teach Yourself* series includes over 300 titles in the fields of languages, crafts, hobbies, business, computing and education.

British Library Cataloguing in Publication Data A catalogue record for this title is available from The British Library.

Library of Congress Catalog Card Number: On file.

First published in UK 2003 by Hodder Headline Plc., 338 Euston Road, London, NW1 3BH.

First published in US 2003 by Contemporary Books, A Division of The McGraw-Hill Companies, 1 Prudential Plaza, 130 East Randolph Street, Chicago, Illinois 60601 USA.

The 'Teach Yourself' name is a registered trade mark of Hodder & Stoughton Ltd. Computer hardware and software brand names mentioned in this book are protected by their respective trademarks and are acknowledged.

Typeset by MacDesign, Southampton

Printed in Great Britain for Hodder & Stoughton Educational, a division of Hodder Headline Plc, 338 Euston Road, London NW1 3BH by Cox & Wyman Ltd., Reading, Berkshire.

Papers used in this book are natural, renewable and recyclable products. They are made from wood grown in sustainable forests. The logging and manufacturing processes conform to the environmental regulations of the country of origin.

Impression number   10 9 8 7 6 5 4 3 2 1

Year   2007 2006 2005 2004 2003

contents

01

web page structure

HTML

HTML stands for HyperText Markup Language, and is the means by which Web pages are created and linked together. It is based on the use of tags. These are key words or phrases which describe how text and graphics are to be displayed, and which create links between different pages or parts of the same page. It is HTML's ability to handle links that makes the Web possible. The World Wide Web is essentially an ever-expanding set of interlinked HTML pages, and a Web browser is essentially a tool that can display these pages and follow up the links embedded in them.

In the first few years of the Web, HTML and browsers were under almost constant development. This put Web page builders into a quandary. If they used features from the latest version of HTML in their pages, people viewing with older browsers would not be able to enjoy them. If you wanted everyone to be able to see your work, you had to keep it simple.

It's different now. HTML reached version 4.0 in 1998 and hasn't changed since. Every browser produced since then is able to handle all HTML 4.0 features, and 95% of people surfing the Web are using one of those newer browsers (Internet Explorer 4.0 or Netscape Navigator 4.0 or later). All of which means that you can take advantage of all that HTML now has to offer, knowing that your visitors will be able to enjoy it to the full.

HTML tags

Tags are instructions to browsers, telling them how to lay out text and what graphics to display where, or carrying links to pages or other files.

Some tags are very simple:

```
<H1>
```

says, 'this text is to be styled as a level 1 Heading' – i.e. use big type.

Some are much more complex:

```
<IMG SRC = "/images/tiddles.gif" ALT = "My cat" WIDTH = 200
HEIGHT = 100 BORDER = 0 HSPACE = 50 ALIGN = left>
```

This tells the browser which picture to display, where and how big to display it, and what text to use instead, if the visitor chooses not to download the graphic.

A few basic rules are common to all:

- Each tag must be enclosed in <angle brackets>.
- You can use lower or upper case letters. These are all the same:

    ```
    <title>
    <Title>
    <TITLE>
    ```

    Upper case is used in this book because it makes tags stand out better from surrounding text.

- Most tags come in pairs – one to mark the start of a style, the other to mark its end. The closing tag has the same keyword as the opener, but starts with a / (forward slash), e.g.

  `<H1>This is a heading</H1>`

- Browsers ignore any spaces or new lines around tags. However, the HTML code will be easier to read if you put spaces around tags, or write them on separate lines. That last example would have been displayed the same on screen if it had been written:

  `<H1>  This is a heading  </H1>`

  or

  `<H1>`

  `This is a heading`

  `</H1>`

Options in tags

Many tags can have optional settings written in them. These
normally take the form:

    OPTION = value

where *OPTION* is the name of the option.

The *value* can be text or numbers, depending upon the option, and
can be enclosed in "double quotes". The quotes are essential if the
value is text containing spaces, but can be omitted from single
words or numbers.

Spaces can be left either side of the = sign, to improve readability,
but are not essential.

For example, these two lines have exactly the same effect:

    <IMG SRC = "dog.jpg" ALT = "My dog" BORDER = "5" ALIGN
    = "left">

    <IMG SRC=dog.jpg ALT="My dog" BORDER=5 ALIGN=left>

The only essential quotes are those around the phrase "My dog".

<IMG SRC ...> is used to display an image. See Chapter 3.

\<HTML\>

Every HTML document starts with the tag:

    <HTML>

and ends with:

    </HTML>

So, at its very simplest, an HTML document might read:

    <HTML>
    This is HTML
    </HTML>

tip

Here's a simple way to explore the tags and techniques from this book. Type the sample code into your word-processor and save it as a **text file**, called *test.htm*, then open the file in your browser to view it. When you come to the next example, re-use *test.htm*, editing it to match the new code, resave it and use **Refresh** to view it in the browser.

<HEAD> and <BODY>

An HTML document has two parts: the head and the body. The head part is enclosed by the tags <HEAD> and </HEAD>. Its contents are not displayed on the screen, and are mainly there to identify the Web page. Style information can be written here (see Chapter 9).

The body is enclosed by the tags <BODY> and </BODY>, and its contents form the displayed page. The <BODY> tag can include options to change the colours of the display or add a background image (see pages 8 and 50).

If you don't have anything to put in the head area, you can miss out the <HEAD> and </HEAD> tags. In fact, on a simple page you can miss out both the <HEAD> and <BODY> tags and it will still work perfectly well.

Here is the simplest, properly-formed HTML page:

```
<HTML>
<HEAD>
</HEAD>
<BODY>
This is HTML
</BODY>
</HTML>
```

<BODY> colours

<BODY BGCOLOR = *value* TEXT = *value* >

You can set the colour of the background and of the text, by
including either or both phrases in the <BODY ...> tag. These
settings apply to the whole document. The colours can be set using
standard names or RGB values.

    <BODY BGCOLOR = yellow TEXT = navy>

Link colours

Text carrying a hyperlink (see page 56) is normally displayed in
blue, if it has not yet been used, or purple if it has. If you change
the colour of the background or the normal text, links may not
stand out as well as you might like.

    <BODY ... LINK = *value* ALINK = *value* VLINK = *value*>

Any or all of these options can be used to set the colour of the text
that leads to:

an unvisited link (LINK),

the active link (ALINK),

a visited link (VLINK).

The colours are set by name or RGB values.

Colour names and values

All screen colours are produced from red, green and blue light in different combinations. By varying the intensity of these three, you can produce the whole range of colours, and the intensity can be varied on a scale of 0 (off) to 255 (full beam). Except to get this full control you have to use hexadecimal. If you do not understand hexadecimal, stick to the standard colour names. If you want to know more about hexadecimal, see page 210.

Name	R	G	B	Name	R	G	B
Black	00	00	00	Red	FF	00	00
Lime	00	FF	00	Blue	00	00	FF
Yellow	FF	FF	00	Fuchsia	FF	00	FF
Aqua	00	FF	FF	White	FF	FF	FF
Maroon	80	00	00	Green	00	80	00
Navy	00	00	80	Purple	80	00	80
Olive	80	80	00	Teal	00	80	80
Gray *	80	80	80	Silver	C0	C0	C0

* Note US spelling

tip

You can use an image as a background. See page 50.

<TITLE>

Every page should have a title. This is not the text that appears at the top of the page – you do that with an <H1> tag. The title is what appears on the title line of the browser window, and what would be used as a bookmark if anyone bookmarked your page.

It is used in the standard way:

```
<TITLE>
Mac's Home Page
</TITLE>
```

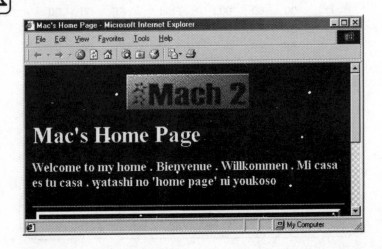

<META>

<META > tags go into the <HEAD> area, and are not visible on the page. They are mainly used to carry information about the page and its author. The basic shape is:

    <META NAME = ... VALUE = ...>

The NAME identifies the nature of the information, and the information itself is the VALUE. For example:

    <META NAME = author VALUE = "Ingrid Bottomlow">

If the VALUE contains more than one word, they should be enclosed in "double quotes".

NAME = Keyword

An important use for <META> tags – and why I have introduced them at this stage – is for carrying keywords. Some of the Internet's search engines will look for these and use them when compiling their databases. The tags should follow the pattern:

    <META NAME = keyword VALUE = "..." >

Keywords are not special words, simply ones that indicate the contents of your page. For example, the Cleethorpes Surfing Club home page might use this keyword tag:

    <META NAME = keyword VALUE = "surfing, water sports, North Sea, frostbite" >

NAME = Classification/Description

Similarly, the classification and description options provide information for search engines and directories. Use them to help people find your site, and to encourage them to visit.

<META NAME="Classification" CONTENT = "sports, water sports, surfing">

<META NAME="Description" CONTENT="The information point for anyone who want to surf the North Sea">

<ISINDEX>

This provides another way to define words or phrases to be picked up by the search engines. Use it in the form:

<ISINDEX PROMPT="Keywords">

The keywords are used in the same way as in the META tags, and could well repeat the information given in there.

<ISINDEX PROMPT = "surfing, water sports, North Sea, frostbite" >

<SCRIPT>

Identifies a block of programming code – normally written in JavaScript. This is a simple but limited language that can add action and interaction to a Web page. JavaScript routines are triggered by events such as the click of a button. The code can be written directly into the tag to which it relates, or as a function in a <SCRIPT> block in the <HEAD> area.

In this example, the <SCRIPT> block contains a function called *showmessage* which displays a prompt box with the caption 'Ouch!'. In the body of the page, you will see this code:

```
<INPUT TYPE = button VALUE = "Click Me" onClick =
"showmessage()">
```

This creates a button, and when it is clicked it calls up the function *showmessage*.

```
<HTML>
<HEAD>
<TITLE>Simple JavaScript</TITLE>
<SCRIPT>
function showmessage() {
 alert('Ouch!')
 }
</SCRIPT>
</HEAD>
```

```
<BODY>
<FORM>
<INPUT TYPE = button VALUE = "Click Me" onClick =
"showmessage()">
</FORM>
</BODY>
</HTML>
```

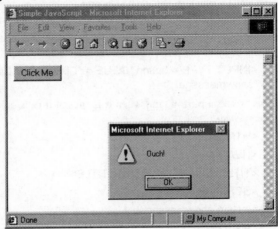

tip

Forms and buttons are covered in Chapter 6.

<APPLET ...>

Java applets are self-contained programs that run within Web pages. They are pulled into the page through the <APPLET> tag which specifies the applet code and sets the size of the display area. To cater for those users who cannot, or do not want to, view applets, alternative text or an image can be included. This example runs the *piano* applet in a 500 × 400 box, or displays the message if the browser cannot handle Java.

```
<APPLET CODE = "piano.class" WIDTH = 500 HEIGHT = 400>

    If you had Java you could play my piano!

</APPLET>
```

It is very satisfying to write your own applets, but learning Java properly is a major undertaking. You may prefer to make use of other people's efforts. The Internet has plenty of ready-written applets which you can adapt to suit your pages – though these tend to carry (prominent and undeletable) adverts for the original author's site.

<PARAM>

Applets can be customized through the use of *parameters*. Values can be passed from HTML to the applet through <PARAM> tags.

<APPLET CODE = banner.class WIDTH = 500 HEIGHT = 200>

<PARAM NAME = message VALUE = "Welcome to my page">

</APPLET>

This applet has two parameters that let you set the message to be displayed. Notice how it caters for browsers that do not support Java – it will display an image, or text, if images are turned off. Ready-made applets that use parameters will also have the relevant HTML code for downloading. All you will need to do is change the text or numbers in the VALUE expressions.

tip

If you want to know more about Java programming, try *Teach Yourself Java* by Chris Wright.

text

02

<H...> headings

There are a set of tags that can be used to define headings over a range of sizes. They all start <H... and followed by a number between 1 and 6.

Type the following into your HTML document, save it and open the file with your browser.

```
<HTML>
<H1> Heading 1 - 24 Point </H1>
<H2> Heading 2 - 18 Point </H2>
<H3> Heading 3 - 14 Point </H3>
<H4> Heading 4 - 12 Point </H4>
<H5> Heading 5 - 10 Point </H5>
<H6> Heading 6 - 7 Point </H6>
Normal body text - 12 Point
</HTML>
```

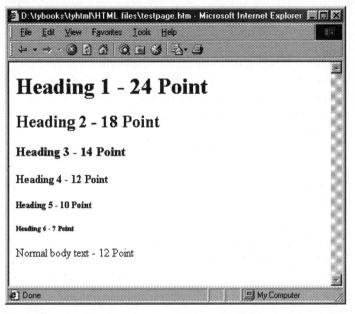

The resulting display should be something like this. Displays vary because the font is determined by the browser, and this can be changed by the user. How you see your file is not necessarily how other people will see it. But, an <H1> heading will always be bigger than an <H2>, and so on down the line.

<P>

This marks the start of a new paragraph, and places a blank line before it. You can equally well place it at the end of a piece of text, at the start of the next, or in between. <P> can be used as a second stand-alone tag, or with a closing </P>.

```
<P>This is a complete paragraph.</P>
<P>
So is this.
<P>And here is a third.
<P>
<P>
<P>And here is the fourth.</P>
```

This produces four equally spaced lines. Extra <P> tags are ignored and the closing </P> is optional.

This is a line BReak and marks the start of a new line.

    Mary had a little lamb

    Its fleece was white as snow

will come out as:

    Mary had a little lambIts fleece was white as snow

To get separate lines you must use

    Mary had a little lamb

    Its fleece was white as snow

Note that <BR> stands alone – there is no closing tag.

<ADDRESS>

These tags have a double effect, setting the text into italic and placing it on a new line. The convention is to use these tags only with your e-mail address. That would normally go at the bottom of your home page.

Edit your HTML test document, or set up a new one, to try out the <TITLE>, <H...> and <ADDRESS> tags. Aim for something along the lines of the one below.

Note the blank lines between sections. They are not necessary – the browser ignores them when it displays the document – but they do make it easier for you to read.

```
<HTML>
<TITLE>Mac's Home Page</TITLE>

<H1>Welcome to my Home </H1>
This page is under construction.

<ADDRESS>macbride@tcp.co.uk</ADDRESS>
</HTML>
```

Adding emphasis

If you want to emphasize a word or phrase in your text, you can use these pairs of tags.

<B> </B>

Sets text to **bold**.

<I> </I>

Makes text *italic*.

<U> </U>

<u>Underlines</u> text – as linked text is also underlined, this should be used carefully, if at all.

<TT> </TT>

This creates a 'typewriter' effect, by setting text in `Courier`.

<S> </S> or <STRIKE> </STRIKE>

~~Strikethrough~~ and this is the first time that I've found a use for it!

<SUP> and <SUB>

<SUP> makes text superscript, <SUB> makes it subscript.

```
<HTML>
<BODY>
 This is <SUB>Subscript</SUB>. This is <SUP>Superscript
 </SUP>.
 <BR>Great for science! E = MC<SUP>2</SUP> H<SUB>2
 </SUB>S0<SUB>4</SUB>
 <H1>They also <SUP>work</SUP> with <SUB>headings
 </SUB>.</H1>
</BODY>
</HTML>
```

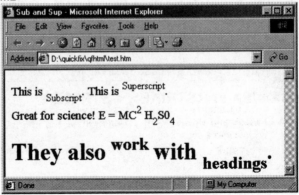

Comments

Every HTML document has two aspects. There is the displayed page that the world will see, and the underlying source code, which is mainly of interest to you. If you want to add comments to the document, for your use and not for general consumption, write them inside <!...> tags, like this:

```
<! Written by me, with help from Harry>
<! Last modified 27/6/2002>
```

tip

If you want to take a tag out of action while you are developing a page, put an exclamation mark at the start to turn it into a comment.

```
<!STRIKE>...check the text before drawing a line through it ...</STRIKE>
```

<FONT SIZE =

The SIZE value can be from 7 down to 1, with 7 the largest size, at 36 points. Size 6 is equivalent to <H1>. Normal body text is size 3.

Note that these values run in the opposite way to <H...> values, where 1 is the largest and 7 the smallest.

For headings, it is simpler to use the <H...> tags – unless you want a huge 36 point heading. Keep the <FONT SIZE = ... > tag for special effects.

To turn off a font size, either set a new <FONT SIZE = ...> or use </FONT> to revert to the previous size.

```
<HTML>
<FONT SIZE = 4> A big <FONT SIZE = 7>Hello </FONT>
from me
</HTML>
```

tip

The tag <SMALL> is the equivalent of <FONT SIZE = 2> and <BIG> is the equivalent of <FONT SIZE = 4>.

Relative sizes

Font size can also be set relative to the current size, using values in the range –4 to +4 (within the standard 1–7 limits).

```
<HTML>
<BODY>
Normal font size
<BR><FONT SIZE = 4>This is size 4 </FONT>
<BR>Back to Normal (size 3)
<BR><FONT SIZE = +2>3 plus 2 makes 5</FONT>
<BR><FONT SIZE = -4>5 minus 4 makes 1</FONT>
<BR>Back to normal
</BODY>
</HTML>
```

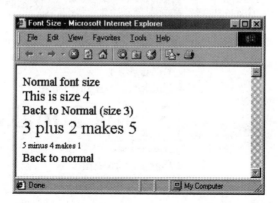

<BASEFONT SIZE = ...>

This changes the size of text at *all* FONT SIZE settings. The default size for normal text is 3. Set the BASEFONT higher than this to make all text larger, or below to reduce all sizes of text.

These screens use the code from page 27, with this line at the start:

    <BASEFONT SIZE = ...>

<BASEFONT SIZE = 1>

<BASEFONT SIZE = 5>

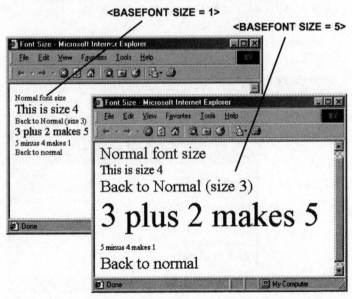

<FONT COLOR =

<FONT COLOR = *value*>

This changes the colour of text, just as <FONT SIZE = ...> sets its size. Likewise, when you have done with a colour, you can switch to a new one with another <FONT COLOR = ... > tag, or restore the previous colour with </FONT>.

Color values are set using the standard names or RGB values (see page 9).

    <FONT SIZE = 6 COLOR = Red>

will give you large red text.

    <FONT SIZE = 1 COLOR = #C0C0C0>

will give you tiny pale grey text, ideal for small print on contracts!

Alignment

Body text and headings are normally aligned to the left edge, but both can be set in the centre or to the right, if required.

To set the alignment, use ALIGN = *Center*, *Right* or *Left* in an <H ...> or <P> tag. (Left is never needed but it can sometimes help to make the coding easier to read.)

For example:

    <H2 ALIGN = Right>

starts a right aligned heading. </H2> closes it.

    <P ALIGN = Center>

makes the following paragraph align to the centre of the window. *Note that the US spelling CENTER must be used in the tags.*

This example demonstrates the ALIGN clause in action.

    <HTML>
    <BODY>
    <H1 ALIGN = Center> Text Alignment</H1>
    <P ALIGN = Center>
    Set in the centre of the window

 As many lines as you like from one ALIGN
    <P> Back to normal
    <P ALIGN = Right> Align to the right
    <P ALIGN = Left> Align to the left. This is the same as not

setting an ALIGN option. Note that long lines wrap round to fit the window size.

```
</BODY>
</HTML>
```

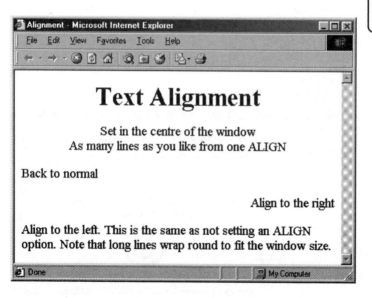

<CENTER>

This is an alternative way to produce centre alignment. After a
<CENTER> tag, everything – text, images or tables will be aligned
in the centre of the screen (unless the ALIGN option is set).

```
<HTML>
<BODY>
<CENTER>
The CENTER tag sets text and images in the centre of the
window
<BR><IMG SRC = smiley.gif>
<P ALIGN = left> But can be overridden by ALIGN settings
</CENTER>
</BODY>
</HTML>
```

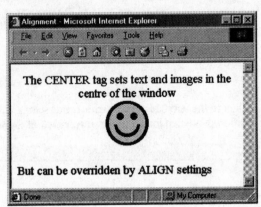

<PRE>

This defines preformatted text, and tells the browser to include the spaces, tabs and new lines, just as they are written. Within the <PRE> block, text is displayed in Courier. Unlike most fonts, Courier does *not* have proportional spacing. Instead every letter and space occupies the same width on screen. This means that you can use spaces to push text over to the right – and get it exactly where you want it. Tags are still obeyed, within the <PRE> block, so you can include headings, font sizes and alignments as usual.

Use <PRE> for price lists, poems, or other text where the pattern of tabs and spaces is important.

In this example, notice the pattern of indents and the right-aligned price list. Note also that the <H...> tags and ALIGN setting produce their usual effects.

```
<HTML>
<BODY>

<PRE>
<H3 ALIGN = "Center"> Rent-a-Rhyme </H3>
    There was a young netter called Seb
    Who put his Home Page on the Web
        He said "What a drag
        I've missed out a tag
    The nerds will all think I'm a pleb"
```

```
<H4>Unbeatable prices!</H4>
    Limericks        4.99
    Clerihews       10.49
    Doggerel            25p per line
    Sonnets         39.99
    Free Verse       £POA
</PRE>
</BODY>
</HTML>
```

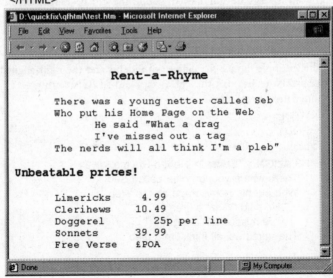

<BLOCKQUOTE>

This is intended for use with quotes and displays text indented from both margins, and with a blank line above and below.

```
<HTML>
<BODY>
Confucius he say:
<BLOCKQUOTE>
If you want to make some text stand out from the page, then
indent it from either side.
</BLOCKQUOTE>
And it works as well on Web pages as it does on scrolls.
</BODY>
</HTML>
```

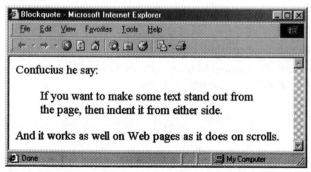

Logical tags

Logical, or phrasal, tags format the appearance of text but are mainly used for marking up text for analysis by other programs.

<ACRONYM TITLE = *full text*> displayed as ordinary text. *full text* is what the acronym stands for and is shown in a pop-up when the mouse is paused over the acronym.

<CITE> used for quotations, displayed in italics.

<CODE> used for samples of program code, displayed in Courier.

<DFN> used for definitions, displayed as normal text.

<EM> used for emphasis, usually displayed in italics.

<KBD> used to indicate keyboard input by user, displayed in Courier.

<SAMP> used for sample outputs from programs, displayed in Courier.

<STRONG> used for stronger emphasis, displayed in bold.

<VAR> used for program variables, displayed in italics.

These can all be redefined using style sheets (see Chapter 9), to provide a neat way of formatting text.

03

graphics

<IMG SRC = >

<IMG SRC ...> (IMaGe SouRCe) links an image into your page.
The basic tag places it against the left edge, directly after any text,
and with later text starting to its right. For example:

```
<HTML>
<H2>Graphics</H2>
<IMG SRC = "ggnome.gif">
The Green Gnome
<P>My brother Gnoggin spends far too much time there!
</HTML>
```

If the file is in the same folder as the HTML document, you only
have to give its name – that was the case here. If the image is stored
elsewhere, you will have to include the path to the folder.

In HTML, the path does not follow Windows rules. HTML was
originally designed for Unix machines and it expects paths written
the Unix way. Use forward slashes not backslashes, between folder
names, and start with a forward slash. Use a vertical bar line (|) and
a slash, in place of the colon after the drive letter.

If you had a graphic MYPIC.GIF in a folder whose Windows path
was C:\WINDOWS\TEMP, its HTML path would read:

```
/C|/WINDOWS/TEMP/MYPIC.GIF
```

That /forward slash at the start is essential.

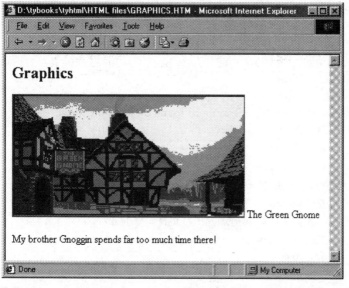

Following text normally starts at the lower right of the image. A <P> tag
will push it onto the next line, or you can use an ALIGN option (page 40).

Keep life simple. Keep the graphics in the same folder as the
HTML files. When you put your page up on the Web, put all
the files into one folder (see Chapter 10).

ALIGN =

Used with images, the ALIGN option sets the vertical position in relation to surrounding text. There are three settings: *Top*, *Middle* and *Bottom*. *Bottom* is the default, placing accompanying text at the bottom of the image.

If there is following text, and it is too long to fit in the remaining space to the right, it is wrapped round to below the image.

```
<HTML>
<BODY>
<H2>Graphics - Alignment</H2>
<FONT SIZE = 4>
Text before
<IMG SRC = "arrows.gif" ALIGN = Middle>
Text after. Long sentences wrap round to below the image
</FONT>
</BODY>
</HTML>
```

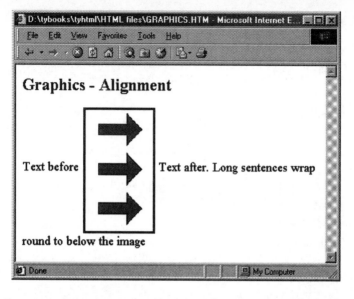

If you want to title an image, an *<H...>* tag will push the heading onto a new line. Use *FONT SIZE* if you want large text beside the image. Where text is so long that it will wrap round below the image, use *ALIGN = Bottom*. As you can see, *ALIGN = Middle* looks a mess and *ALIGN = Top* is even worse! Alternatively, use a table to set a block of text beside an image (Chapter 7).

<CENTER>

<CENTER> can also be used as a tag in its own right to align text and graphics in the centre of the display window. When used in this way, a closing </CENTER> tag is needed at the end of the centred material.

For example:

```
<HTML>
<BODY>
<H3>Positioning Graphics</H3>
<CENTER><IMG SRC = "smiley.gif"></CENTER>
</BODY>
</HTML>
```

If this had been written:

```
<HTML>
<BODY>
<CENTER>
<H3>Positioning Graphics</H3>
<IMG SRC = "smiley.gif"></CENTER>
</BODY>
</HTML>
```

both the heading and image would have been centred.

ALT text

This is the text that appears when you pause the mouse over an image, or what is shown if the image is not displayed. It is also the text that will be read by the screen-readers used by the visually-impaired.

ALT text should give a brief but clear description of the image.

```
<IMG SRC = adonis.gif ALT = "Photo of me">
```

Space around images

There are two options that can control the spacing around graphics. The default settings are to leave a space of 10 pixels above and below an image, and about 6 pixels to either side.

HSPACE = sets the spacing (in pixels) to the left and right;

VSPACE = sets the spacing above and below the image.

You cannot control left and right, or above and below spacing independently.

```
<HTML>
<BODY BGCOLOR = 80FF80 TEXT = 00008F>
<IMG SRC = "arrow1.gif" ALIGN = Middle> Buy now! <P>
<IMG SRC = "arrow1.gif" ALIGN = Middle> Huge savings!<P>
<IMG SRC = "arrow1.gif" ALIGN = Middle VSPACE = 25>
Unrepeatable bargains!! <P>
<IMG SRC = "arrow1.gif" ALIGN = Middle HSPACE = 50>
Don't miss it!!!!
</BODY>
</HTML>
```

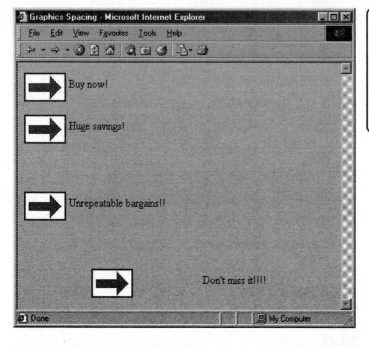

Unless you are aiming for a particularly 'spaced-out' look, the HSPACE and VSPACE values should not be too large. In this example they have been exaggerated so that their effects are clearly visible. Compare the bottom two with the top two graphics, which are placed at the default spacing.

BORDER =

You can put a border around an image by including the option
BORDER = ... setting the thickness in pixels. e.g.

    <IMG SRC = "mypic.gif" BORDER = 5>

If the image is used in a hyperlink (see Chapter 4), it will normally
be given a 1 pixel border in the same colours that are used for
linked text. This could be turned off by setting the border to 0.

    <A HREF = www.hardtofind.com> <IMG SRC = "htf.gif" ALT =
    "Link to HardToFind Inc." BORDER = 0>

tip

You cannot set the border colour. It will always be black,
unless the image is carrying a hyperlink, in which case it will
be the colours that are used for unused, active or visited links.

HEIGHT and WIDTH

You can set an image size in two alternative ways:

- fixed, where the displayed size is given in pixels;
- variable, where the size is specified as a percentage of the screen height or width.

The advantage of the variable approach is that you can be sure that your image will fit on screen, whatever the size of your visitors' windows. We'll come back to that in our second example.

For **fixed** sizing, simply give the pixels as plain numbers:

HEIGHT = 100   WIDTH = 75

sets the displayed size of the image at 100 x 75 pixels. If you want to avoid distorting the shape, you must know the original pixel size, so that you can calculate the new values.

For **variable** sizing, give the value as a percentage of the screen height *or* width, and follow the number with a % sign.

HEIGHT = 50%

sets the image to be scaled down so that it fills half the height of the browser window.

WIDTH = 25%

scales the image down to fit into a quarter of the width of the window.

If you only set one value, the same scaling is applied in both directions. Set HEIGHT *and* WIDTH only if it is essential that the image occupies a certain amount of space in both directions – you can guarantee that few of your visitors will be using the same shape of browser window as you, so that most will get a distorted image.

```
<HTML>
<BODY BGCOLOR = FFFFFF>
<IMG SRC = "compass.gif"> Original size 60 x 60
<IMG SRC = "compass.gif" HEIGHT = 90 WIDTH = 90>
Increased to 90 x 90 <BR>
<IMG SRC = "compass.gif" HEIGHT = 50%> Sized to fill half
of the screen height <BR>
<IMG SRC = "compass.gif" WIDTH = 10%> Sized to fill a
tenth of the width
</BODY>
</HTML>
```

tip

There is little point in showing an image at a reduced size – you may as well make it smaller to start with, and save that image to file. If you make the display larger than the original, it keeps down the size of the file and the download time, but it will produce a lower resolution image. This won't matter if the original picture was simple and chunky anyway, but is not advisable for photographs or scanned art.

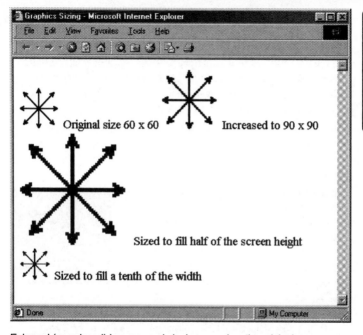

Enlarged (or reduced) images rarely look as good as the originals.

Background images

Another striking use for an image is as a background to your page. The trick here is *not* to use a large, full-page picture – which will take an age to download – but to use a small image. HTML automatically repeats any image used as a background, so you can get a full screen from the tiniest images.

With any kind of background pattern, it is important that the pattern does not become too dominant – it is supposed to be a background after all. The answer is either to use a very sparse pattern, or pale colours. You can see examples of both here.

The screen on the next page has a 'deep space' background, formed by repeating this scatter of stars. The original image is about 200 pixels square, and as a GIF file, takes less than 500 bytes. Used with bright yellow or cyan text, it is striking, but still produces a readable page.

```
<HTML>
</HEAD>
<BODY>
<BODY BACKGROUND = "stars.gif" TEXT = FFFF00>
<FONT SIZE = 7> One for the Star Trek fans
<FONT SIZE = 5>
<P> The simpler the background, the better
</BODY>
</HTML>
```

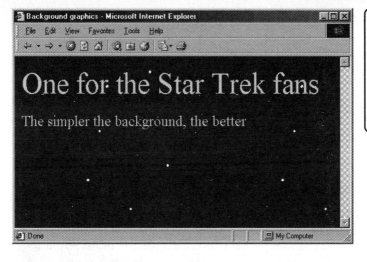

tip

The only file formats that can be handled by all browsers are GIF (Graphic Information Format) and JPEG (Joint Photographic Experts Group). GIF files can only handle 256 colours, which is fine for drawings and cartoons. For photographs you should use JPEGs, which can cope with 16 million colours. Built-in compression keeps their file size down.

<HR>

HR stands for Horizontal Rule and draws a line. It is a stand-alone tag. The basic line is two pixels deep, almost the full width of the window, and has a shaded effect. These can be changed by options.

SIZE = *value*

This sets the thickness of the line, in pixels. It must be at least 2 if you want a shade effect. Over about 8 pixels, it looks less like a line than a box.

WIDTH = *value*

This sets the width of the line. As with the WIDTH of images, you can set it in pixels or as a percentage of the browser window's width. Unless you want the line to match a heading or image, or you are creating a pattern, it is usually best to set the width as a percentage. You then get the same effect, whatever size window it is viewed in.

ALIGN = *value*

This sets the line to the left, right or in the centre of the screen. It can only be used if the width has been set.

NOSHADE

If this keyword is used, a solid line is drawn.

You can see the effect of setting the options in this example. Try it for yourself – and with other values.

```
<HTML>
<BODY>
<H2> Horizontal Rules </H2>
<H3>Size and Shading</H3>
<HR SIZE = 1>
<HR SIZE = 2>
<HR SIZE = 8>
<HR SIZE = 8 NOSHADE>

<H3>Width and Alignment</H3>
<HR WIDTH = 50>
<HR WIDTH = 100 ALIGN = center>
<HR WIDTH = 300 ALIGN = right>
<HR WIDTH = 50% ALIGN = left>
</BODY>
</HTML>
```

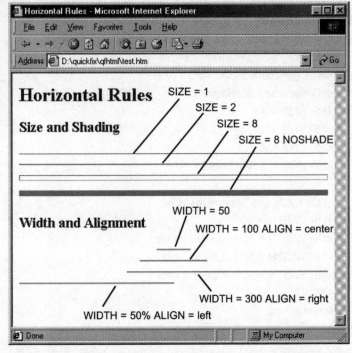

Some of the possible effects you can get with the <HR> options. The first line in the Size set is only 1 pixel deep – note that it is not shaded. In the Width set, the first two lines are too small to be significant if used alone, but can be combined with longer lines to good effect.

links

04

<A HREF = ...>

HREF (Hypertext REFerence) is the key word for hyperlinks – or *links*, for short. This identifies the target page, or point within a page. But it can't be used by itself. It must be anchored to a piece of text or a graphic, so that there is something to click on to pick up the link. The *anchor* tags are <A ...> and </A> which mark the start and end of the link text or image.

The two are used together to create the link and its jumping off point. For example:

<A HREF = "http://www.yahoo.com"> Go to Yahoo </A>

Let's break that down:

<A HREF =   marks the start of the tag.

http://   identifies it as a World Wide Web link. You could miss this out and the link would still work. But if you want any other type of link, you must include the identifier (see opposite).

www.yahoo.com   the URL of the target – this is the home page of the Yahoo! directory.

Go to Yahoo   is the link text that is underlined in the browser, and can be clicked to connect to the URL.

</A>   marks the end of the link text.

You can use different types of links, and replace the text by an image, but all hyperlinks follow this pattern.

URLs

Every page, file, directory, site and person on the Internet has its
URL – Uniform Resource Locator. The basic pattern is the same:

type://HostComputerAddress/Directory/Filename

Type	Identifiers
http://	Web page
file://	file in a local directory
ftp://	file that can be downloaded via FTP
news://	link to a newsgroup
mailto://	e-mail address of a person

On the Internet, hard disks are said to be divided into
directories; in Windows they are divided into *folders*. It is just
jargon! Directories and folders are the same things.

Links to pages at other sites

The simplest links are to the home pages of sites. These just need
http:// (you can even miss it out) and the site address. e.g.

    <A HREF = "http://www.google.com"> Google </A>

If you are linking to a page in a subdirectory, or to the home page of
an individual user, you must get the page address absolutely right –
using upper and lower case and punctuation exactly according to
the URL. In particular, watch out for:

- the use of underlines and capital letters

  http://www.yahoo.com/Computers_and_Internet

  this is the Computers and Internet menu at Yahoo.

- tildes (~), used to indicate an individual user's page

  http://homepages.tcp.co.uk/~macbride/tybooks.html

  my 'Teach Yourself books' page at Total Connectivity Providers.

Links within your web site

Web pages are best kept small so that they download quickly and so that the reader doesn't have to scroll through many screenfuls to get to the part they want to see. If they are all interlinked properly, visitors will be able to navigate quickly around the set.

The pages should all be stored in the same folder – now, on your system while you are testing them, and later when you upload them to your service provider. The link is then a very simple one, consisting only of the filename:

```
<A HREF = "tiddles.htm"> My Cat's Home Page </A>
```

The linked pages should have a link back to the top-level page.

Here's a skeleton set for a simple system:

The top level. Filename = *index.html*

```
<HTML>
<BODY>
...
<A HREF = "myjob.htm"> My Job </A>
<A HREF = "myhobby.htm"> My Hobby </A>
<A HREF = "links.htm"> Favourite Places </A>
<A HREF = "author.htm"> All about me </A>
...
</BODY>
</HTML>
```

Linked page. Filename = *myjob.htm*

```
<HTML>
<HEAD>
<TITLE> My Job </TITLE>
</HEAD>
<BODY>
I work for .......
<A HREF = "index.html"> Return to the top </A>
</BODY>
</HTML>
```

Links into folders

Files are easiest to handle if they are all in the same folder, but if you have to link to pages, graphics or any files in other folders, here are the rules.

If the file is in a subfolder of the one holding the page that calls for it, use the pattern *folder_name/filename*:

    <A HREF = "holiday/snapbook.htm">

finds the *snapbook.htm* page in the *holiday* subfolder.

To get back up from a subfolder, use double dots (..). e.g.

    <A HREF = "../index.htm">

will take you back to the index page in the folder above.

To link to a file elsewhere on the system, you have to give the full path, from the root, down to the folder. The path starts with a forward slash, to specify the current system, and you must use a vertical bar (|) and a slash, in place of the colon after the drive letter. For example:

    <A HREF = "/C|/graphics/gallery.htm">

When you upload your files to your service provider, check first with them to find the correct path to your place in their system.

Links within a page

If you want to jump from one part of a page to another, you can define the jump points with a variation on the anchor tag:

<A NAME = *jumppoint*> jump point text </A>

The *jumppoint* can be a single word or phrase. It is not identified in the display – there is no reason to do so, as this is a place that you arrive at, not somewhere to go from. The <A NAME = ...> tag can be wrapped around a heading, or set in body text at the right place.

Here are two examples:

<A NAME = "my job"> I work </A> for .....

<A NAME = "backup"> Welcome </A>

At the jumping-off point, use an HREF tag, as with other links:

<A HREF = #*jumppoint*> text </A>

Notice the hash (#) before the *jumppoint* name. It is crucial. If you miss it out, the browser will think that you are trying to make a simple link to another page in your directory.

As with other links, it is vital to use exactly the same punctuation and upper/lower case characters in the HREF as in the NAME.

<A HREF = #Me> All About Me </A>

will not find:

<A NAME = "me"> I am </A> nearly 9 and have surfed for...

because "me" and "Me" are two different things.

Jump points on other pages

If you want to be very precise in your linking to other pages, you can set up a link to a NAMEd jump point in another page.

`<A HREF = "cats.htm#tiddles"> Go to Tiddles corner </A>`

This will link to the *cats.htm* page, jumping to the *tiddles* part of it.

Jump point references can be added to links to other pages elsewhere on the Web, as long as you know the NAME. This will jump-link to the updated links section of my *Teach Yourself HTML* page:

`<A HREF = "homepages.tcp.co.uk/~macbride/tybooks#links">`

…assuming that I haven't changed the page by then.

Links and images

Links can be anchored to graphics, replacing the text with an <IMG SRC = ...> tag. For example:

    <A HREF = www.MyFirm.com> <IMG SRC = logo.gif> </A>

That would create a link to your firm's home page (if it was called My Firm), based on the image of your logo. Look for the image link in this next example.

    <HTML>
    <BODY>
    <H2>Welcome to Cleethorpes</H2>
    <A HREF = meggies.html> <IMG SRC = meggies.gif ALT =
    "How to get there"></A>
    <P><A HREF = surfsup.htm> Surfing the North Sea </A>
    <P><A HREF = tweet.htm>The Budgie-Fancier's Paradise</A>
    </BODY>
    </HTML>

Notice the ALT text in the image. If a visitor has image loading turned off, they will see this:

A linked image is normally outlined in the same colour as that used for linked text. If you do not want the outline, set the option BORDER = 0 in the <IMG SRC ...> tag.

Multimedia links

Browsers cannot display audio and video clips, but they can pass them to other software to be played. There are a number of file formats, and visitors may not have a suitable player to view your clips. AVI and WAV files can be handled by the Windows 95/98 Media Player. The XP Media Player can also display the newer and more efficient WMA and WMV formats. If you are using other file types, you should included a link to a Web site where your visitors could find the necessary viewing software.

Multimedia files are pulled into a page with the HREF link.

```
<A HREF = "newwave.avi"> New video from the hottest rock
group in Neasden (959Kb) </A>
```

```
<A HREF = "jo walks.wmv"> Jo's first steps (725Kb) </A>
```

Do include the file size in the accompanying text so that visitors know what to expect – multimedia clips tend to be large and slow to download.

If you intend to use clips, do check that your service provider allows you enough Web storage space. Some of the less generous providers restrict their users to as little as 1Mb of space, which will not go far if you are into multimedia.

mailto: links

The *mailto:* facility gives a simple means for your visitors to contact you by e-mail. It will call up the mail composition window in Outlook Express (or whatever e-mail software your visitors use), with your address in the **To:** slot, ready for them to write a message to you.

    <A HREF = mailto:jobloggs@yournet.co.uk> Mail me! </A>

Your visitor can then complete the subject line and message, and send it as normal.

tip

If you want structured feedback from your visitors, use a form
– see Chapter 6.

Image maps

An image map is a graphic that has a number of separate areas, each carrying a different link. There are two ways of producing an image map. The easy way is to get a bit of software to do the job for you; the hard way is to do it yourself – though even that is not so hard.

Any graphic can be used, as long as it is a GIF file. It can be a photograph or scanned image, an integrated design or a collection of small images on a common background (as in the example used here). Text can be added if desired. All that is essential is that your visitors should be able to identify where they should click and what will happen when they do that.

If you are setting up the image map by hand, you will need to go over the image and note the co-ordinates of the top left and bottom right corners of the areas that hold each clickable part.

```
<HTML>
<BODY BGCOLOR=Black TEXT=White LINK=Yellow
VLINK=Aqua>
<P ALIGN = CENTER>
<IMG SRC="imagemap.gif">
</P>
<A HREF="machome.htm">Mac </A> *
<A HREF="tylogo.htm">Teach Yourself </A> *
<A HREF="ingrid.htm">Ingrid's Home Page </A> *
```

```
<A HREF="soton.htm"> What's on in Soton </A>
</BODY>
</HTML>
```

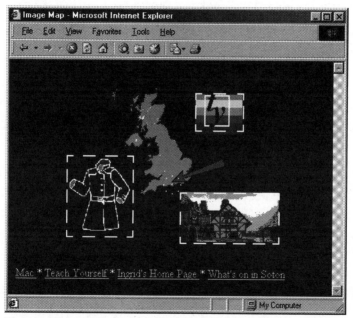

The example map page, showing the clickable areas – these are not outlined on the actual image. You should also have text links to the same places, so visitors can still get there, even if they choose not to load images.

<MAP...> and <AREA...>

To make a graphic into an image map, we add the option USEMAP to give it a name. This must be a single word and start with #.

    <IMG SRC = mymap.gif USEMAP = #mymap>

This name is picked up at the start of the mapping section, which is marked by the <MAP NAME = ...> tag.

    <MAP NAME = mymap>

Note that the # is omitted here. The use of # in map names reflects its use in the names of jump points.

Inside the <MAP ...> section, you define each area of the map which is to carry a link. The definitions look like this:

    <AREA SHAPE = "rect" COORDS = "15,120,115,240" HREF
    = "machome.htm">

Let's break that line down into its parts:

<AREA	marks the start of the tag;
SHAPE =	either *rect*, *circle*, *polygon* or *default*
COORDS =	are the co-ordinates that define the shape.
HREF = ...>	the URL of the page to be linked to the area.

Mark the end of the <MAP ...> section with the tag </MAP>.

Co-ordinates

The pattern of co-ordinates depends upon the shape:

for *rect*, give the top left and bottom right corners; e.g.

    COORDS = 25, 25, 100, 75

for *circle* give the centre, followed by the radius; e.g.

    COORDS = 200, 50, 25

for *polygon*, give the x,y co-ordinates of each point, working round
the shape and back to the start: e.g.

    COORDS = 100, 100, 200, 100, 150, 50, 100, 100

The background can be referred to as *default*. You can link a page to
here, or if you do not want this to be linked, set it to NOHREF.

    <AREA SHAPE = "default" NOHREF>

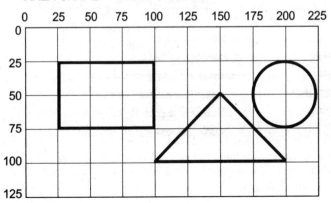

MapEdit

If that last section has left you feeling that there ought to be an easier way to set up image maps, then this section is for you. MapEdit, from Boutell Inc., is a simple, effective and cheap ($25 in 2003) solution. Get an evaluation copy from them at:

http://www.boutell.com/mapedit

MapEdit is available for Windows, Apple Mac, Linux and Unix systems. Select the one you need and download it from their home page. It comes in as a small self-extracting ZIP file – the latest Windows version is just under 280Kb.

To use MapEdit, first prepare your map image and place it in an HTML document – any required text or text links can also be added at this stage. Save the document and run MapEdit.

Give the **File > Open** command, and at the **Open** dialog box, browse for the HTML file containing your map.

MapEdit will scan the file and pick up any image references. You will then be asked which one to map. (The document could have any number of images in it – for that matter, you could set up several maps on different images in one document.)

Once the image is loaded in, you can start to create clickable areas on it. Select a shape tool, then click the top left corner and drag and click on the bottom right corners for a rectangle, click the centre and drag and click to the edge for a circle, or click the sequence of points for a polygon.

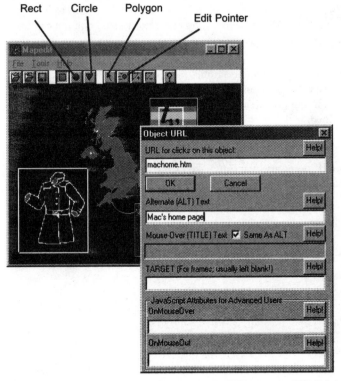

Rect   Circle   Polygon   Edit Pointer

Object URL

URL for clicks on this object: Help!

machome.htm

OK   Cancel

Alternate (ALT) Text   Help!

Mac's home page

Mouse-Over (TITLE) Text ☑ Same As ALT   Help!

TARGET (For frames; usually left blank!)   Help!

JavaScript Attributes for Advanced Users
OnMouseOver   Help!

OnMouseOut   Help!

If afterwards you need to change a shape, or its URL, use the Edit Pointer
to select the area then make your alterations.

After the last click, MapEdit asks for details of the URL to be linked to that area. ALT text, for visitors who don't load graphics, can be defined at this stage, and if you are working in frames, you can also set the TARGET for the linked page to be displayed in.

As you add areas, their outlines remain visible – these will not be displayed in the working map. Shapes can overlap, but note that a click in the overlap area will select the first area to have been defined.

When you have finished, save the file. If you then open it in your word-processor, you will see that MapEdit has written the code for you. If necessary, you can make further adjustments or addition 'by hand'.

05

lists

Bulleted lists

A bulleted list is enclosed by <UL> and </UL>.

Each item in the list is preceded by <LI> (List Item).

For example:

```
<H4>Our Gold Star service includes</H4>
<UL>
 <LI>Free delivery
 <LI>No quibble 'Return if not delighted'
 <LI>Bio-degradable packaging
 <LI>Special 2 for the price of one offer on Garlic bread
</UL>
```

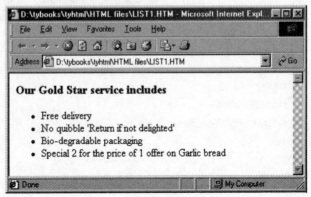

Bullet types

With a plain <UL> tag, the bullets are filled circles. The TYPE
option lets you set the bullet style. The alternatives are:

square a filled square;

disc a filled circle (the default bullet);

circle an open circle.

```
<HTML>
<BODY>
<H3>Our Gold Star service includes</H3>
<UL TYPE = square>
<LI>Free delivery
<LI>No quibble 'Return if not delighted'
<LI>Bio-degradable packaging
<LI>Special 2 for the price of one offer on Garlic bread
<H4>Toppings</H4>
<LI>Pepperoni
<LI>Black Olives
<LI>Mushrooms
<LI>Ham and Pineapple
</UL>
</BODY>
</HTML>
```

Nested lists

Lists can be 'nested', one inside the other, to give you several levels of indents. The same tags are used as for simple lists – but you must put a </UL> tag at the end of each inner level. Note that you can use different bullet styles for the inner and outer lists.

```html
<HTML>
<BODY>
<H3>Our Gold Star service includes</H3>
<UL TYPE = square>                    ———— outer list start
<LI>Free delivery
<LI>No quibble 'Return if not delighted'
<LI>Bio-degradable packaging
<LI>Special 2 for the price of 1 offer on Garlic bread
<LI>With all your favourite toppings
    <UL TYPE = disc>                  ———— inner list start
    <LI>Pepperoni
    <LI>Black Olives                  inner list items
    <LI>Mushrooms
    <LI>Ham and Pineapple
    </UL>                             ———— inner list end
</UL>                                 ———— outer list end
</BODY>
</HTML>
```

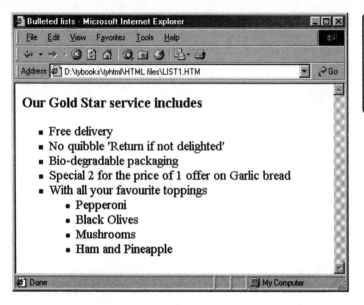

tip

When writing nested lists, if you indent your inner list items in the code it shows the structure more clearly, and makes it easy to do a quick check that each opening <UL> tag has a matching </UL>.

Numbered lists

Numbered lists follow exactly the same rules as bulleted lists, but here the tag is <OL>.

A simple <OL> produces normal numbers. The TYPE options are:

I   Roman capitals, I, II, III, IV

i   Roman numerals, i, ii, iii, iv

A   capital letters, A, B, C

a   lower-case letters a, b, c

The TYPE options can be useful in nested lists. For example:

```
<HTML>
<BODY>
<H2>Things to do</H2>
<OL TYPE = A>                        Level 1 list A,B,C
<LI>Clean out the Guinea Pigs
  <OL TYPE = I>                      Level 2 list, I, II, III
  <LI>Fetch the hay
  <LI>Push the pigs out of the way
  <LI>Shovel the old stuff where Pa won't fall in it
  </OL>                             End of level 2
<LI>Make some real bread
  <OL>                             Level 2 list, 1, 2, 3
```

```
<LI>Buy some yeast
  <OL TYPE = i>                    ——————    Level 3 list, i, ii, iii
  <LI>Try the village shop
  <LI>Try Seamus Sosmall
  </OL>  ——————————      End of level 3
<LI>Light the stove
<LI>Get baking!
  </OL>  ————————
  </OL>                End of level 2
</BODY>
</HTML>          End of level 1
```

tip

If you are nesting lists, you can use bullets for one level and
numbers for another. A bulleted outer list and a numbered
inner list can be a very effective combination. You can change
the FONT SIZE, or use <B>, <I> and other emphasis tags or
headings to make some levels of text more or less prominent.

Level 1 (A, B, C)

Level 2 (I, II, III)

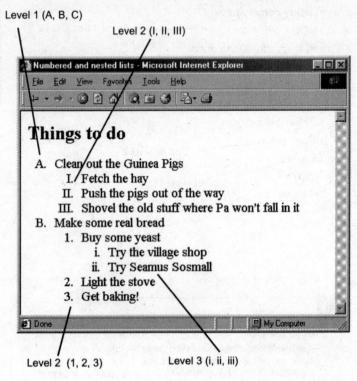

Level 2 (1, 2, 3)

Level 3 (i, ii, iii)

Definition lists

These are intended for lists of terms and definitions, but serve equally well for any set of text items where you want a series of sub-headings with following text. The tags are **<DL>**, **</DL>**, **<DT>** and **<DD>**, and their meanings are explained in the next example.

The <DL> and <DD> lines of text appear in the same font size and style – unless you format them otherwise – but <DD> lines are indented one tab.

You can have several <DT> or <DD> tags in succession if you have terms without definitions or several definitions for one term.

```
<HTML>
<BODY>
<H2> List tags </H2>
<DL>
  <DT> &lt DL &gt
  <DD> marks the start of the list
  <DT> &lt DT &gt
  <DD> identifies a term
  <DT> &lt DD &gt
  <DD> identifies the definition
</DL>
</BODY>
</HTML>
```

See the tip on page 84 for an explanation of these

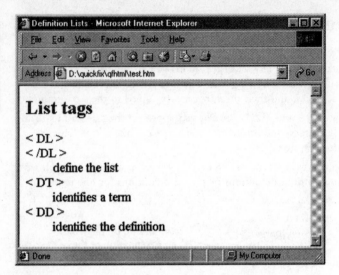

List tags

< DL >
< /DL >
    define the list
< DT >
    identifies a term
< DD >
    identifies the definition

tip

The symbols '<' and '>' have special meanings in HTML. If
you want them to appear in your text, substitute these
expressions:

   <   < (less than)   >   > (greater than)

There are more symbols that have to be replaced in the same
way. See the list of special characters on pages 212–13.

Fancy bullets

You can create fancy bulleted 'lists' by fitting your own images at
the starts of lines. These are not proper lists, as defined by <OL> or
<UL> tags and they take more work, but the results are worthwhile.

Create the bullet image in Paint. Select the image, and use **Edit >
Copy To...** to save it to file. Convert this to a GIF and save it in
your HTML folder.

Now to build the list. There are three things to bear in mind:

- We need an image at the start of every item line.
- To create an indent, we will need to set the HSPACE value in
  the <IMG SRC ...> tag.
- The items must be on separate lines – and <BR> will give a
  shallower break than <P>.

The resulting source code is not as compact as a standard list!

```
<HTML>                        A graphic is used here as the heading
<BODY>
<CENTER><IMG SRC = top5head.gif ></CENTER>
<P>
<IMG SRC = redbtn.gif HSPACE = 20><A HREF = http://
www.yahoo.com>Browse at Yahoo</A> <BR>
<IMG SRC = redbtn.gif HSPACE = 20><A HREF = http://
www.lycos.com>Browse at Lycos</A> <BR>
```

```
<IMG SRC = redbtn.gif HSPACE = 20><A HREF = http://
www.google.com>Search at Google</A> <BR>
<IMG SRC = redbtn.gif HSPACE = 20><A HREF = http://
www.altavista.com>Search at AltaVista</A> <BR>
<IMG SRC = redbtn.gif HSPACE = 20><A HREF = http://
www.msn.co.uk>MSN's UK site</A>
</BODY>
</HTML>
```

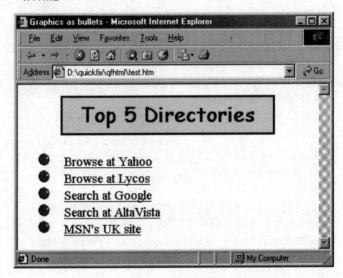

06

forms

<FORM>

A form can be written on a page of its own, or be included within a larger page. It can include the normal range of text, lists, images, links and other objects, but it can also include the tags that will collect data and send the form.

The start of the form is marked by the <FORM> tag, and will contain the two keywords METHOD and ACTION. These can each take several options, and the simplest is this:

    <FORM METHOD = Post ACTION = mailto:your_address>

With these settings, the data entered into the form is e-mailed to you when the form is submitted.

Within the form, data is collected mainly in <INPUT ...> tags. There are a number of options that can be used here. The most important is NAME = ... which sets up a *variable* – a place to store data input by your visitor.

    <INPUT NAME = email>

This creates the variable *email*. It will be displayed on screen as a blank data entry slot, 20 characters wide. For a different size slot, add the option SIZE = ..., giving the number of characters.

Put some text nearby, so your visitors know what it is for:

    E-mail address: <INPUT NAME = email SIZE = 30>

A second option that you must know about is one that sets up a button to send the form's contents back to you.

The basic shape:

```
<INPUT TYPE = Submit VALUE = "Send Now">
```

The phrase: TYPE = Submit defines it as a button that submits feedback. VALUE = "Send Now" defines the button's caption. You can use any text you like, but you must enclose it in quotes or only the first word will be displayed.

You now have enough to produce a simple feedback form, e.g.:

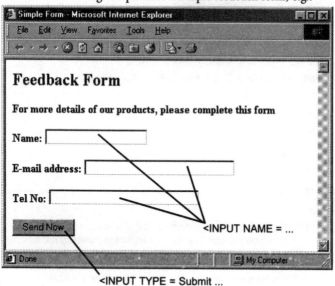

```
<INPUT NAME = ...
```

```
<INPUT TYPE = Submit ...
```

And here's the code that you need:

```
<HTML>
<BODY>
<H2> Feedback Form </H2>
<FORM METHOD = Post ACTION = your_address>
<B>
For more details of our products, please complete this form <P>
Name: <INPUT NAME = Visitor> <P>
E-mail address: <INPUT NAME = Email SIZE = 30> <P>
Tel No: <INPUT NAME = Phone SIZE = 30> <P>
<INPUT TYPE = Submit VALUE = "Send Now">
</B>
</FORM>
</BODY>
</HTML>
```

tip

Forms involve two-way communication and will only function if your service provider is able to process the incoming data. This should not create a problem – all they have to do is run some standard software to pick up the feedback. If your ISP cannot handle feedback from forms, give them a nudge.

Understanding feedback

When someone submits your form, it is mailed to you automatically. When you next check your mailbox, you will then find an entry labelled 'Form posted from Internet Explorer'. Open it, and there should be an attachment. Look at that in a text editor and you will see something like this:

Surname=Bill+Gates&Email=bgates@microsoft.com&Phone=...

This may look a bit messy, but is easily turned into a more readable form. Use a word processor to replace each + by a space and each & by a new paragraph, and you have this:

Surname=Bill Gates

Email=bgates@microsoft.com

Phone=...

If you are marketing a business on the Web, and expect lots of feedback, talk to your service provider. Most can set things up so that replies are collected, collated into a more usable form and mailed out once a day.

Checkboxes and radio buttons

If you want your form-fillers to be able to choose from a set of
alternatives, you can have:

☑ Checkbox where several alternatives can be chosen, or

◉ Radio, where only one of the set can be selected.

They are created using the TYPE option and are used in similar
ways, with one significant exception. With checkboxes, each
INPUT should have its own NAME variable, to store the response.

> I am interested in:
> <INPUT TYPE = Checkbox NAME = hard> Hardware
> <INPUT TYPE = Checkbox NAME = soft> Software
> <INPUT TYPE = Checkbox NAME = books> Books <P>

If the visitor selects the *Hardware* checkbox, the variable *hard* will
have the value *on*.

With radio buttons, the same NAME is used for all the buttons in
the set, as you only want to allow one of the alternatives to be
chosen. But we now need to add the VALUE = clause. This sets the
value to be returned, so that the feedback will be in the form of
set_name = radio_value. If you omit the VALUE =, the feedback
would read *set_name = on*, whatever was selected.

> Sex:
> <INPUT TYPE = Radio NAME = sex VALUE = m> Male

```
<INPUT TYPE = Radio NAME = sex VALUE = f > Female <BR>
<INPUT TYPE = Radio NAME = sex VALUE = dk CHECKED>
Don't Know
```

The keyword CHECKED in the last <INPUT...> sets the default.
Miss it out if you want to start with all the radio buttons clear.

Compare this HTML code with the following screen display.

```
<HTML>
<BODY>
<FORM METHOD = Post ACTION = mailto://sales@clogs.com>
Tell me more about these wonderful Witherspoon clogs <P>
Style: <BR>
<INPUT TYPE = Checkbox NAME = trad> Traditional <BR>
<INPUT TYPE = Checkbox NAME = slipon> Slip-on<BR>
<INPUT TYPE = Checkbox NAME = gold> Gold Lame<P>
Sex: <BR>
<INPUT TYPE = Radio NAME = sex> Gents<BR>
<INPUT TYPE = Radio NAME = sex CHECKED> Ladies <P>
<INPUT TYPE = Submit VALUE = "Send">
<INPUT TYPE = Reset VALUE = "Clear and Restart">
</FORM>
</BODY>
</HTML>
```

**See the note on the next page
about the Reset button**

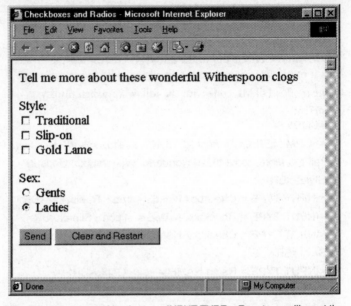

A Reset button, created by the tag <INPUT TYPE = Reset ...> will reset the selections and clear any data entered into a form, in case the visitor wants to start again.

Textareas

The simple <INPUT ...> only accepts one line of text. If you want to collect more than this, use a textarea, like this:

```
<TEXTAREA NAME = Comments>
```

This displays as a (very) small box with scroll bars to the right and bottom. To make it bigger, add the options ROWS and COLS to set the size. The one in this screenshot was produced by these lines:

```
Address: <BR>
<TEXTAREA NAME = Address ROWS = 4 COLS = 40>
</TEXTAREA>
```

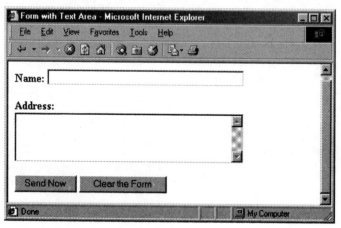

Three things to note here:

- The <BR> after the prompt text places it above the text area. If you miss this out, to put the prompt to the left, it aligns with the bottom of the textarea and looks a mess.

- The ROWS and COLS settings only affect the display size. If your visitors want to write more lines, or longer ones, they can – that's what the scroll bars are there for.

- <TEXTAREA ...> needs a closing </TEXTAREA> tag – even though there should be nothing between the two tags.

Drop-down lists

Drop-down lists are a neat way of offering a long set of alternatives. They are created with the tags <SELECT ...> and <OPTION =...>

<SELECT ...> provides the framework for the list. It takes the keyword NAME to define the variable where the selection will be recorded. The matching tag </SELECT> closes the list.

<OPTION = *value*> defines an entry. The *value* will be fed back to you in the SELECT NAME variable. It must be followed by a label to be displayed in the list. You need an <OPTION = ...> tag for every item.

The tags fit together like this:

```
<SELECT NAME = Level>
 <OPTION = stand> Standard
 <OPTION = prof> Professional
</SELECT>
```

That gives us a drop-down list with two items.

If the visitor selects *Standard*, the *stand* option will be passed to *Level*, and the feedback mail will include this phrase:

```
Level = stand
```

An <OPTION = ...> tag can include the word SELECTED, to set that item as the default.

Look for the line:

```
<OPTION = Win SELECTED> PC/Windows
```

in this next example, and notice how the item *PC/Windows* is displayed at the top of the list, in the selection slot – though its natural place is further down.

```
<HTML>
<BODY>

<H2> Order Form </H2>
<FORM METHOD = Post ACTION = mailto:sales@pcs.co.uk>
Order your software here: <P>

Platform: <SELECT NAME = Platform>
 <OPTION = Pcdos > PC/DOS
 <OPTION = Mac> Mac
 <OPTION = Unix> Unix
 <OPTION = Win SELECTED> PC/Windows
</SELECT>

Level: <SELECT NAME = Level>
 <OPTION = stand> Standard
 <OPTION = prof> Professional
</SELECT>

<P>
```

```
<INPUT TYPE = Submit VALUE = "Send" >
</FORM>
</BODY>
</HTML>
```

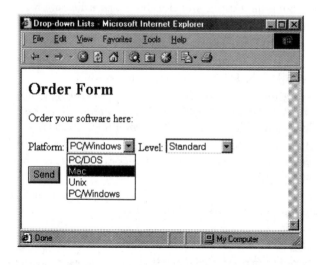

<LABEL>

This tag creates an active link with an <INPUT> field, so that selecting the label selects the field. It works with all <INPUT> types, but is most useful with checkboxes and radio buttons.

```
<INPUT TYPE = Radio NAME = sex ID = male>

<LABEL FOR = male> Gents </LABEL>
```

Notice that the <INPUT> tag has the option ID = ... which is picked up by the FOR = ... option in the <LABEL>.

The <LABEL> looks like plain text – until you click on it, when it takes a dotted outline. Clicking a <LABEL> turns on its associated radio button or checkbox (or turns it off if it was on already).

A <LABEL> can be written before or after its linked <INPUT>. Obviously, this changes the relative positions on the screen, but it doesn't make any difference to how it works.

Here's the checkboxes and radio buttons example again, with the plain text prompts made into <LABEL>s.

```
<HTML>

<BODY>

<FORM METHOD = Post ACTION = mailto://sales@clogs.com>
Tell me more about these wonderful Witherspoon clogs <P>
 Style: <BR>
 <INPUT TYPE = Checkbox NAME = trad ID = trad>
 <LABEL FOR = trad> Traditional </LABEL> <BR>
```

```
<INPUT TYPE = Checkbox NAME = slipon ID = slip>
<LABEL FOR = slip> Slip-on </LABEL><BR>
<INPUT TYPE = Checkbox NAME = gold ID = gold>
<LABEL FOR = gold> Gold Lame </LABEL> <P>
```

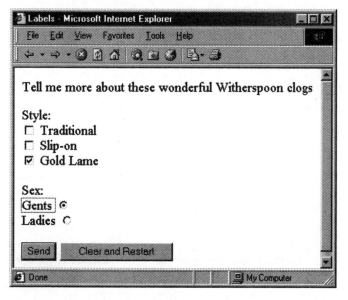

The only way that you can tell the difference between a plain text prompt
and a <LABEL> is by clicking on it.

```
Sex: <BR>
<LABEL FOR = male> Gents </LABEL>
<INPUT TYPE = Radio NAME = sex ID = male> <BR>
<LABEL FOR = female> Ladies </LABEL>
<INPUT TYPE = Radio NAME = sex CHECKED ID = female>
<P>
<INPUT TYPE = Submit VALUE = "Send">
<INPUT TYPE = Reset VALUE = "Clear and Restart">
</FORM>
</BODY>
</HTML>
```

<BUTTON>

The <BUTTON> tag is an alternative to <INPUT TYPE = reset/ submit>. If all you want is a standard 'Submit', there is no advantage in using this. These two lines produce identical results:

```
<BUTTON TYPE="submit"> Send me </BUTTON>
```

Send me

```
<INPUT TYPE = "submit" VALUE = Send me>
```

Send me

The point about the <BUTTON> tag is that you have more control over what appears on the button. You can format the text:

```
<BUTTON TYPE="submit"><FONT SIZE = 5 COLOR = red>
<B> Send me </B></FONT></BUTTON>
```

This gives you large, bold, red characters on the button.

Send me

You can even use an image instead of text...

```
<BUTTON TYPE="submit"> <IMG SRC = "sendme.gif">
</BUTTON>
```

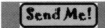

...or as well as text:

```
<BUTTON TYPE ="submit"> <FONT SIZE = 6> Send me
please</FONT> <img src = "smiley.gif"></BUTTON>
```

Send me please ☺

Submit image buttons

There is a special <INPUT TYPE = ...> option that is worth
knowing about.

```
<INPUT TYPE = "image" SRC = "sendme.gif">
```

Send Me!

This displays the image, but makes it work as a submit button. The
advantage of this is that it does not have the standard grey, rectan-
gular background, which you get with <BUTTON>, but it can only
be used for submitting forms.

CGI scripts

The ACTION = mailto: ... method does not work with some older browsers. If you want to make sure that all your visitors are able to mail the form, you need to use a CGI script. And for this you need the co-operation of your Internet service provider.

CGI is a programming language, devised for use on the Internet. Its scripts (programs) can only be run on suitable servers, such as the computers at your service provider. Most providers have several ready-made ones that you can use, and amongst these there should be one which will handle feedback from forms. The scripts are normally straightforward to use – a few adjustments to your form should be all that is needed.

Here is how you would use the feedback script at my service, Total Connectivity Providers. Theirs is the *formmail* script, by Matt Wright. Yours may use the same one, or something similar – but check with them before you go much further.

The <FORM ACTION... line calls up the script:

```
<FORM ACTION = "http://www.tcp.co.uk/cgi-bin/formmail"
METHOD = "POST">
```

Within the form, you must have a *recipient* field, which holds your e-mail address, so that the script knows where to mail the feedback. You don't want this to appear on the form, so it must be hidden.

Here's what the line should look like:

```
<INPUT TYPE = "hidden" NAME = "recipient" VALUE =
"your_address">
```

Your form will normally include fields for your visitor's e-mail address and real name. If you would like this information to be included in the **From:** line of the message, when the script mails it to you, those fields should be called *email* and *realname*.

```
<P>Name: <INPUT TYPE = text NAME = "realname">
```

```
<P>E-mail address:
```

```
<INPUT TYPE = text NAME = "email" SIZE = 30>
```

The rest of the form is identical, whether it is being returned to you by an ACTION=mailto: or by a CGI script.

Do check with your service provider before starting on this. It is possible that they do not have a facility for running scripts, and even more likely that their scripts are used in a different way from the one described here.

70

tables

The basic tags

For a simple table, you only need three pairs of tags, used in this pattern:

```
<TABLE>
<TR>
    <TD> Column item </TD>
    <TD> Column item </TD>
    ... across the columns
</TR>

<TR>
    <TD> Column item  </TD>
    ... across the columns
</TR>
... down all the rows
</TABLE>
```

The table is built from the top left, working across the columns. Each item is enclosed in <TD> </TD> tags, and each row in <TR> </TR> tags. It takes a lot of tags to make a big table!

Here's a simple table. The first row has two items – 'Earth' and 'Air', the second row has 'Fire' and 'Water'.

```
<TABLE>
   <TR>
      <TD> Earth </TD>
      <TD> Air </TD>
   </TR>
   <TR>
      <TD> Fire </TD>
      <TD> Water </TD>
   </TR>
</TABLE>
```

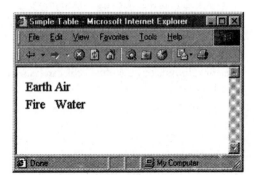

Indenting rows by one tab space and items by two makes the code easier to check – you can run your finger down it making sure than each <TR> has a matching </TR>.

Table backgrounds

A table is normally transparent, so that the background colour or image shows through.

You can give a table a distinctive background in two ways:

    <TABLE BGCOLOR = colour>

Sets the background colour. Colours are specified as for BODY backgrounds (see page 9).

    <TABLE BACKGROUND = filename>

Sets an image as a background. If the image is smaller than the table, it is repeated to fill the space, just as a BODY background image is (see page 50).

The backgrounds of individual cells can be set in the same ways:

    <TD BGCOLOR = colour>

    <TD BACKGROUND = filename>

Borders

Adding a border is easy and improves the look of tables. For a simple border, include the keyword BORDER in the <TABLE> tag.

    <TABLE BORDER>

The default settings are to have a thin line around each item and one around the whole table, a narrow space between the inner and outer borders, and the text close to the edge of the inner borders. The latter three settings can be changed.

BORDER can take a value, setting the thickness of the outer border. The value is given in pixels, e.g.:

    BORDER = 10

CELLSPACING = ... sets the distance, in pixels, around the border of each item.

CELLPADDING = ... sets the distance, in pixels, between the inner border and the text.

The options are all set in the <TABLE ...> tag:

```
<TABLE BORDER = 10 CELLSPACING = 10
CELLPADDING = 20>
```

CELLSPACING and CELLPADDING can be omitted – they are then set at 5 pixels.

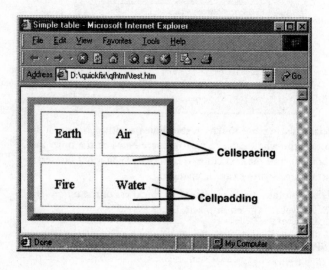

Border colours

When you start to thicken borders, you realize that the top and left border are lighter than the right and lower lines, giving a 3-D effect. The colours normally used are silver and dark grey. These can be changed by setting the options BORDERCOLORLIGHT and BORDERCOLORDARK.

```
<TABLE BORDER = 10 BORDERCOLORLIGHT = blue
BORDERCOLORDARK = navy>
```

This produces bright and dark blue borders.

```
<TABLE BORDER = 10 BORDERCOLORLIGHT = maroon
BORDERCOLORDARK = red>
```

This colours the borders light and dark red, but swaps the shading over.

tip

If you set the BORDER width to 0, the borders disappear but the table is still there to provide a framework for holding images and text. We can use this to create newspaper style columns and other interesting layouts.

FRAME

These **BORDER** options give you fine control over which borders are displayed.

FRAME defines the outer border. There are eight settings:

void – no border (this is the default value)

above – top border only

below – bottom border only

hsides – horizontal (top and bottom) borders only

vsides – vertical (right and left) borders only

lhs – left-hand side border only

rhs – right-hand side border only

box or *border* – all four borders

So to draw a 5-pixel border above and below the table but not round the sides:

```
<TABLE BORDER=5 FRAME=HSIDES>
```

RULES

RULES defines the lines around the cells. The five possible settings:

none – no rules

groups – rules between row groups and column groups only (see pages 124–6 for more on groups)

rows – rules between rows only

cols – rules between columns only

all – rules between all cells.

If a cell does not have any content, rules will not be drawn around it, whatever the setting.

Width and position

The WIDTH option lets you set the width of the table. It can be set in pixels or as a percentage of the browser window width.

    <TABLE WIDTH = 50%>

Sets the table to be half the width of the browser window.

    <TABLE WIDTH = 600>

Sets the table to be 600 pixels wide.

The ALIGN controls the position of the table within the window. The default is to the left. The settings are *left, right, center*.

In this example the settings are:

    <TABLE WIDTH = 80% ALIGN = center>

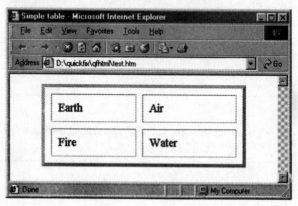

<CAPTION>

Use this to add a (bold) caption. It will be aligned centrally with the
table and is normally placed above the table. You can use the option
ALIGN = bottom to place it below. The caption text must be closed
with </CAPTION>.

<CAPTION ALIGN = bottom>A table of the elements

</CAPTION>

The caption code can be *written* anywhere inside the <TABLE> tags
– but the text will always appear above the table, or below if the
ALIGN = bottom option is used.

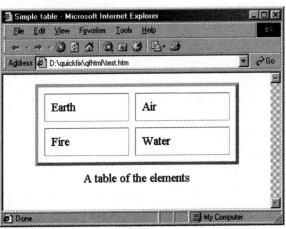

<TH>

This marks a heading, to a row or column within the table. It is used like a <TD> tag, but sets the text in bold and aligns it in the centre of its cell. Close the heading with a </TH> tag.

The next table has headings for the rows and columns. Note the empty one at the start to create that blank cell in the top left.

```
<HTML>
<BODY>
<TABLE BORDER = 5 CELLSPACING = 5 CELLPADDING = 5>
<CAPTION>
<H4>Up and Away Holidays</H4>
</CAPTION>
   <TR>
      <TH> </TH>
      <TH> Florida </TH>
      <TH> Malaga </TH>
      <TH> Tuscany </TH>
   </TR>
   <TR>
      <TH> 7 nights </TH>
      <TD> £479 </TD>
      <TD> £399 </TD>
```

A blank <TH> tag produces an unbordered space

```
         <TD> £359 </TD>
      </TR>
      <TR>
         <TH> 14 nights </TH>
         <TD> £629 </TD>
         <TD> £519 </TD>
         <TD> £539 </TD>
      </TR>
</TABLE>
</BODY>
</HTML>
```

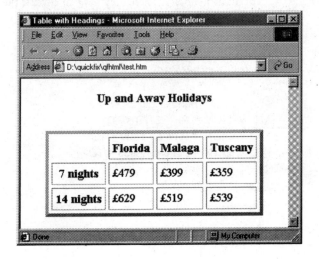

Alignment in cells

Normally <TH> headings are aligned in the centre of their cells, both vertically and horizontally, and <TD> items are aligned to the left, in the middle of the space. If needed, these can be changed.

These options apply to both <TH> and <TD> tags.

ALIGN =   can take the values *Left*, *Center*, or *Right* to set the horizontal alignment.

VALIGN =   can take the values Top, Middle or Bottom to set the vertical alignment. These only have an effect if the row is deeper than the items.

Here's another version of the last table, with alignments set for the top row.

The relevant part of the code reads:

```
<TR>
    <TH ALIGN = right> 7 nights </TH>
    <TD VALIGN = Top> £479 </TD>
    <TD VALIGN = Middle> £399 </TD>
    <TD VALIGN = Bottom> £359 </TD>
</TR>
```

ROWSPAN and COLSPAN

Not all tables fit into a simple grid. One which held a mixture of images and text, for example, may need to span two or more rows or columns with one item. Both <TH> headings and <TD> items can be extended across or down the cells with the options:

ROWSPAN = to set the number of rows deep

COLSPAN = to set the number of columns across

e.g.

```
<TD COLSPAN = 3>
```

extends the cell across three columns. You would then omit the next two <TD> tags for that row.

```
<TD ROWSPAN = 2>
```

makes the cell two rows deep. If you do this, you should omit the corresponding <TD> tag on the next row.

In this example, the cells that hold the round table images are set to span two rows, and the one holding the long table spans two columns. Adapt the code to use your own images and text.

```
<HTML>
<BODY>
<TABLE BORDER=5 CELLPADDING=5>
  <TR>
    <TD>Tables made to order</TD>
```

```
        <TD ALIGN=center><IMG SRC="TABLE1.gif">
      </TD>
      <TD>Summer sale now on! </TD>
   </TR>
   <TR>
      <TD ALIGN=center ROWSPAN=2>
        <IMG SRC="TABLE2.gif"></TD>
      <TD ALIGN=center><H2>The King Arthur</H2>
        </TD>
      <TD ALIGN=center ROWSPAN=2>
        <IMG SRC="TABLE2a.gif"></TD>
   </TR>
   <TR>
      <TD><B>A round table for nights of dining
        pleasure. In dark or light oak</B></TD>
   </TR>
   <TR>
      <TD><H2>The Great Hall</H2>
      This refectory table is ideal for the larger family. In 3m,
        5m and 6m lengths </TD>
      <TD ALIGN=center COLSPAN=2>
        <IMG SRC="TABLE3.gif"> </TD>
   </TR>
```

```
    </TABLE>
    </BODY>
    </HTML>
```

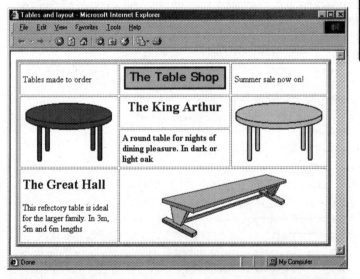

The basic table here is four rows by three columns. The left and right cells of the second and third rows have been merged. In the bottom row, the middle and right cells have been merged. Compare the code to the screenshot to see how the COLSPAN and ROWSPAN options are working.

<THEAD> <TFOOT> <TBODY>

These tags group the rows of a table into three sections – head, body and foot. They are mainly intended for marking up tables so that other programs can interpret them, converting information into a database format, for example, or printing out large tables, with headers and footers on each page.

They can also be useful from a design angle, as they can take the same background and alignment options as the <TABLE> tag, allowing you to format each section separately.

- <THEAD…> marks the group of rows which make up the table head
- <TFOOT…> for the foot
- <TBODY…> for the body – and a table can have more than one <TBODY> section

Each of these tags is then followed by <TR> and <TD> tags which define cells and their contents in the usual way.

The <THEAD…> and <TFOOT…> come first, so that the browser can start to lay out the table without reading all the body rows – there could be hundreds!

```
<HTML>
<BODY>
<TABLE BORDER=1 WIDTH = 90% ALIGN = center>
<THEAD BGCOLOR=orange ALIGN=center VALIGN=bottom>
```

```
   <TR>
      <TD>Title</TD> <TD>Author</TD> <TD>Pub Date</TD>
   </TR>
<TFOOT BGCOLOR=lime ALIGN=right>
   <TR>
      <TD COLSPAN=3>From Hodder & Stoughton</TD>
   </TR>
<TBODY BGCOLOR=cyan>
   <TR>
      <TD>QuickFix HTML</TD> <TD>Mac Bride</TD>
      <TD>2003</TD>
   </TR>
<TBODY BGCOLOR=yellow>
   <TR>
      <TD>Teach Yourself Java</TD> <TD>Chris Wright</TD>
      <TD>2002</TD>
   </TR>
   <TR>
      <TD>Teach Yourself C++</TD> <TD>Richard Riley</TD>
      <TD>2002</TD>
   </TR>
   </TABLE>
</BODY>
</HTML>
```

<COLGROUP>

This is allows you to format a group of columns together. The <COLGROUP> tag is placed immediately after the <TABLE...> tag, before any data, to define column widths and formats so that the browser knows how to set out the table from the start. The options include those for alignment and background and these two:

- **SPAN** determines how many columns the group contains
- **WIDTH** sets the default width of each column in the group.

The following code sets up a table with 6 columns; the first at 200 pixels wide, and the other 5 at 10% of the browser window each:

```
<TABLE>
   <COLGROUP WIDTH=200>
   <COLGROUP SPAN=5 WIDTH=10%>
   <THEAD>
      <TR>...
```

<COL...>

Within a group, you can format individual columns with the <COL...> tag, perhaps to set a different alignment or background.

If there are any <COL> tags, the **SPAN** option is ignored and the <COL> tags counted instead. So if you want to format just one column in a group, you must add empty <COL> tags before and after it to keep the right number of columns.

```
<HTML>
<BODY>
<TABLE BORDER=1 ALIGN = center>
<COLGROUP WIDTH = 120>
<COLGROUP SPAN = 2 WIDTH = 15% ALIGN = center>
   <COL BGCOLOR = cyan>
   <COL BGCOLOR =yellow ALIGN = left>
<COLGROUP WIDTH = 100>
<THEAD BGCOLOR=orange ALIGN=center VALIGN=bottom>
   <TR>
      <TD>Language</TD>   <TD>Teach Yourself</TD>
<TD>QuickFix</TD><TD>Author</TD>
   </TR>
<TFOOT BGCOLOR=lime ALIGN=right>
   <TR>
      <TD COLSPAN=4>From Hodder & Stoughton</TD>
   </TR>
<TBODY>
   <TR>
      <TD>HTML</TD> <TD>Yes</TD> <TD>Yes</TD>
      <TD>Mac Bride</TD>
   </TR>
```

```
<TR>
    <TD>Java</TD> <TD>Yes</TD> <TD>No</TD>
    <TD>Chris Wright</TD>
</TR>
<TR>
    <TD> C++</TD> <TD>Yes</TD> <TD>No</TD>
    <TD>Richard Riley</TD>
</TR>
</TABLE>
</BODY>
</HTML>
```

**Backgrounds set in <THEAD>, <TFOOT>
or <TBODY> tags override those in
<COLGROUP> or <COL>**

08 frames

The frame concept

With frames, you have two distinct types of document:

- *Layout documents* create the frames. They normally carry no displayed content whatsoever – their function is purely to divide the window up into areas.
- *Content documents* go into the frames. They are identical to normal pages, though you may need to adjust their links if the pages are to call each other up within the frame window.

A layout document can divide a window into any number of frames, either vertically or horizontally – but not both. However, a frame can hold another layout document, which can subdivide either vertically or horizontally. The nesting of frames within frames can go on ad infinitum, but in practice you do not want more than three layout documents or four content frames in one page – it would be just too confusing for both you and your visitors.

In the diagram opposite, **Layout 1** contains two frames:

    Content 1

    Layout 2 containing two frames

        Content 2A

        Content 2B

A good way to use your frames is to have one that displays your logo, title or other identifier – this would stay on show permanently. A second frame will hold an index or contents list which

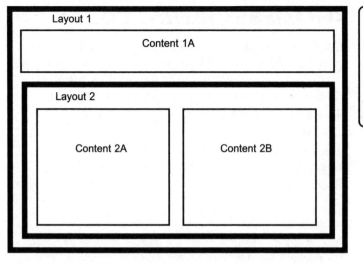

allows your visitors to navigate through the set of pages that are displayed in the third frame. A large or complex site might have several contents lists which could be switched into the second frame to give access to different sets of pages.

The frame structure does not have to remain fixed. You can load a new layout document into a frame, or into the whole window, to give a different structure – and to link to new sets of contents documents.

<FRAMESET ROWS / COLS = ...>

This defines the division of the window into frames. It can take either the ROWS or the COLS option depending upon which way you want to divide. You must specify the size of every division.

The size can be given as fixed, percentage or relative values.

Fixed defines the width or depth of a frame in pixels:

    ROWS = 150, 300...

makes the first row 150 pixels deep, and the second row 300.

Percent sets the width or depth as a percentage of the browser window size:

    COLS = 25%, ...

makes the first column take 25% of the width of the frame.

Relative sets the width or depth as a fraction of the remaining area. The symbol '*' used by itself simply means all the rest of the space:

    ROWS = 200,*

sets up two frames, the first 200 pixels deep, the second taking up whatever space is left below.

* can also mean 'fraction', when used with a number.

    COLS = *, 3*

says, 'divide the window into two columns, with the second being 3 times as wide as the first'. It has the same effect as ...

    COLS = 25%, 75%

* is useful where you have a mix of fixed and percentage sizes:

ROWS = 100, 25%, *

This creates three horizontal frames. The top one is 100 pixels deep, the second is 25% of the window height, and the third is whatever space is left.

</FRAMESET>

This closes the frame definition. Between <FRAMESET...> and this you define the contents of the frames using <FRAME ...>.

tip

Some browsers cannot handle frames. If you want to cater for these, use <NOFRAMES> – see page 136.

<FRAME SRC = ... >

This is where you specify the page to be placed into the frame, e.g.

    <FRAME SRC = banner.htm>

If the frame is to be used as a *target* – i.e. to display pages, which will be linked from another frame, it will need a name:

    <FRAME SRC = toppage.htm NAME = showplace>

This frame will display the *toppage.htm* file when it first opens, then be used to display linked pages. We'll return to this on page 137.

The tag can take some options to define the nature of the frame.

    NORESIZE

fixes the size of the frame.

    SCROLLING = *Yes/No/Auto*

forces scrollbars to be on, off or turned on as necessary.

These two layout documents creates a three-frame system, with a banner across the top, links down the left and a main display area. First split the window horizontally:

```
<HTML>
<FRAMESET ROWS = 100,*>
  <FRAME SRC = banner.htm NORESIZE SCROLLING = No>
  <FRAME SRC = inframe.htm SCROLLING = Auto>
</FRAMESET>
</HTML>
```

Then split the lower frame vertically, saving the file as *inframe.htm*.

```
<HTML>
<FRAMESET COLS = 30%,*>
  <FRAME SRC = navigate.htm>
  <FRAME SRC = content.htm NAME = contents>
</FRAMESET>
</HTML>
```

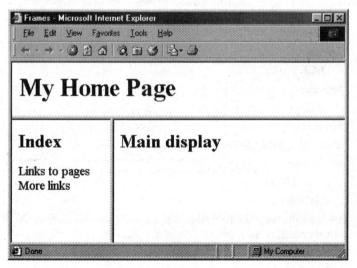

Here is the output, with temporary text in the *banner.htm*, *navigate.htm* and *content.htm* files.

<NOFRAMES>

Frames cannot be handled by old browsers (IE 3.0 and earlier).
There are no longer many of these around, but if you want to cater
for them, use the <NOFRAMES> tags. These can be used, inside
the <FRAMESET ...> tags, to enclose text and other material to be
displayed on browsers that cannot handle frames.

The best use for a <NOFRAMES> section is to direct visitors to a
no-frames version of the site.

```
<HTML>
<FRAMESET ROWS = 100,*>
    <NOFRAMES>
    This page uses frames. <BR>
    Click <A HREF = index1.htm> here </A> for the
no-frame version.
    </NOFRAMES>
... other frame stuff ...
</FRAMESET>
</HTML>
```

Browsers that can handle frames will simply ignore the code in the
<NOFRAMES> area.

Links and targets

Normally when you create a link, there is no question as to where the new page is displayed – it replaces the calling one. When you have frames, there is a question of where to display the linked page. The answer is supplied through an option in the <A HREF ...> tag.

<A HREF = "url" TARGET = ...>

Using frames, you have five alternative targets – places in which a linked page can be displayed.

TARGET =

framename	displays in the frame identified as framename in its <FRAME SRC = ... NAME = *framename*> tag.
_self	displays in the current frame. If you miss out the **TARGET** phrase, it has the same effect.
_parent	replaces the layout document containing the linking frame, with the new page – which may well be a new layout document, giving a new structure.
_top	replaces the top level layout document, i.e. the whole window, with the new page.
_blank	opens a new copy of the browser and displays the page in there. You can have as many browser windows running at once as you like!

For example:

    <A HREF = myclub.htm TARGET = mainframe>

This displays the *myclub* page in the *mainframe* frame.

    <A HREF = newframe.htm TARGET = _parent>

replaces the current layout document with the *newframe* one.

09

style sheets

What are style sheets?

Style sheets were introduced with HTML 4.0, and give us far more
control over our displays. They can be used for the normal text and
paragraph formatting, but also for controlling:

● text size and spacing – between letters, words and lines;

● margins, borders and background colours for the page and for
paragraphs;

● the way images appear in the background of a page, and the use
of images as bullets for lists.

There are a number of style sheet languages, each extending HTML
in its own special way. The most important of these is CSS1 –
Cascading Style Sheets, version 1. Its standards have been imple-
mented in Internet Explorer and Netscape Navigator, from version
4.0 onwards, and that's the only one we need to know about.

Style sheets work by allowing you to redefine tags. For example, you
could redefine <H1> so that text enclosed in this tag was displayed
in Arial, coloured red and centre aligned instead of Times, black
and on the left.

It is a 'cascading' system because you can have any number of style
sheets in a page – a 'style sheet' is simply a definition of one or more
styles – and formatting is passed on from one sheet to the next.

The <P> tag, for instance, might have styles applied to it at three
points in a document. The first style sheet might set the colour, font

size and margins; the second set the margins; the third set the colour and background colour. The final display will take the font size from the first, margins from the second and its colours from the third style sheet.

With multiple style sheets and restyling you can set different formats within a document. In large organizations, you can have one style sheet to set the basic common format for the whole site, a second to set the variations for a department, a third to set a special format to suit an individual document, and further restyling within it to pick out particular items.

Specifying style sheets

There are three ways that you can set up a STYLE:

- write the style specifications in a STYLE block – the main way that we will be using;
- use the STYLE keyword within a tag to redefine it, e.g.
  ```
  <P STYLE="color: blue">This paragraph is blue.</P>
  ```
- link to or import an external style sheet (see page 175).

`<STYLE>` blocks

A STYLE block consists of the `<STYLE>...</STYLE>` pair enclosing a set of styling lines. The block can be written anywhere in the document, but is normally placed in the **HEAD** area. It can be written in the BODY area, but must be `<!commented out>` to stop it being displayed by older browsers.

Here's a simple **STYLE** block:

```
<STYLE TYPE=text/css>
    H1 { text-align:center; color: red }
</STYLE>
```

TYPE = **text/css** specifies the language – *Cascading Style Sheets*.

A style definition starts with a tag name – without `<brackets>` – followed by one or more styles given as '*attribute:format*', separated by semi-colons and enclosed in {curly brackets}.

The *attribute* defines which aspect of the style to set, and the *format* says how it should look. Spaces can be used freely within the definition to improve readability – they are ignored by the browser. The example above redefines `<H1>` to be centred and red, but it keeps the default font and size as these have not been redefined.

There are around 50 attributes and nearly 100 format options, but they are not things that you will normally use very often – look them up in the summary (page 206) when you need them!

Elements and inheritance

In style sheet jargon, an *element* is a tag and the text or image affected by it. The BODY itself, an <H…> heading, a <P> paragraph, a <B>bold</B> item within a block of text – all are elements.

An element within another, such as bold text within a paragraph, is the *child* of the containing element – which is its *parent*. And children inherit characteristics from their parents. So, if the <P> tag has been defined as blue, 14 point, the <B> bold text is also blue and 14 point – unless these formats have been redefined by styling the <B> tag.

The following code shows inheritance at work. Focus on how styles are inherited and overriden – we'll get back to the details of formatting shortly.

- The **BODY** style sets yellow text on a red background.
- **P** sets the background to blue and centre-aligns the text.
- **H1** redefines the font name but takes the text colour from the **BODY** setting.
- **B** sets the text to white and upper case but retains its parent background colour – red within untagged text and blue within the P element.

```
<HTML>
<HEAD>
<TITLE>Inheritance</TITLE>
```

```
<STYLE type=text/css>
    BODY {background-color:red; color:yellow}
    P {background-color:blue;text-align:center}
    H1 {font-family: arial, sans-serif}
    B {color:white; text-transform:uppercase}
</STYLE>
</HEAD>
<BODY>
<H1>Inheritance</H1>
```

Untagged text takes the <B>body</B> style - yellow on a red background, and left-aligned by default.

<P>Inside a P tag, the P style settings override those set at BODY level, the background is now blue and the text centre-aligned.</P>

<P>An element inside another is its child <B> and may have a child of its own. </B> B inherits the blue background from P but has changed the text to red and upper case.</P>

```
</BODY>
</HTML>
```

<P> blue background, centred

<B> white, capitals

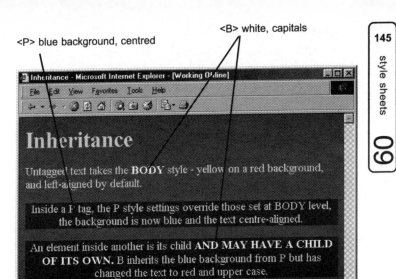

Fonts

A <FONT FACE = > tag will fail if the font is not present on the browser that is viewing the page. The *font-family* attribute gets round this by allowing you to give a list of alternatives, which should end with a generic name. When the page is viewed, the browser will work through the list and use the first named that it can, or otherwise use one of the generic type.

Font names should be written as they appear in your system, enclosed in "double quotes" if there are spaces in the name.

The generic names are:

serif (e.g. Times New Roman)

sans serif (e.g. Arial)

cursive (e.g. *Lucida Calligraphy*)

fantasy (e.g. Playbill)

monospace (e.g. Courier New).

This line sets the <P> text to a sans serif font, preferably Arial or Helvetica.

    P {font-family: arial, helvetica, sans-serif}

Font style, weight and size

font-style

This can be *italic*, *normal* or *oblique*.

font-variant

This can be set to *normal* or *small-caps*.

font-weight

This gives you levels of 'boldness'. It can be set by:

the keywords *lighter*, *normal*, *bold* or *bolder*,

or by the numbers 100, 200, 300 ... to 900, with 500 being normal and 900 the heaviest type.

font-size

This can be set in three ways:

the keywords *xx-small*, *x-small*, *small*, *medium*, *large*, *x-large* or *xx-large* (equivalent to HTML sizes 1 to 7),

or *larger* or *smaller* (set the size relative to the parent element),

or by a percentage based on the line-height (see page 152).

e.g. to make the H2 headings italic, a fairly heavy bold, size 5:

    H2 {font-style:italic; font-weight:700; font-size:large}

Text colour

The **color** attribute sets the colour of the text. It can be given using
the standard colour names (see page 9), the hexadecimal values or
the expression **rgb(*red_val, green_val, blue_val*)**, or by

    BODY {color:white}
    B {color:FF8000}
    P {color:rgb(192,0,192)}

These set white as the default colour for text and borders, orange
for bold text, and lilac (lots of red and blue, but no green) for the
paragraph text.

tip

When setting colours using the **rgb(*red,green,blue*)** method,
the intensity of each colour should be in the range 0–255,
where 255 is brightest. It is actually the same as defining
colours with hexadecimal values, but with normal numbers.

Font example

When working with the next example, try different size, weight and font family settings to see the effects. Also, try defining different attributes within the <B STYLE = ...> tag. You should see that those that could have an impact outside the tag – e.g. weight and size – cannot be redefined.

```
<HTML>
<HEAD>
<TITLE>Formatting Fonts</TITLE>
<STYLE type=text/css>
    BODY {font-family: "Lucida Sans", Helvetica, sans-serif}
    H1 {font-family: "Lucida Calligraphy", cursive; font-size:x-
        large}
    H2 {font-style:italic; font-size:16pt}
    P {font-family:Georgia, "Times New Roman",serif; font-
        size:14pt; font-weight:400}
    B {font-weight:bolder}
</STYLE>
</HEAD>
<BODY>
<H1>Formatting Fonts</H1>
<H2>Set the face, size, and <B>style</B></H2>
```

Remember that if you don't use P tags, <B>text takes the BODY style</B>.

<P>And that within any tags you can restyle an element <B STYLE = color:red> - even within the tag itself</B>

</BODY>

</HTML>

Body text

Body text with added <B> setting

Here the <B> text is made red by the
new STYLE embedded in the code

<P> text

Special text fomats

text-decoration

This draws lines across text and has three settings:

   underline – the same as the <U> tag;

   line-through – the same as the <STRIKE> tag;

   overline – special to style sheets.

text-transform

This sets the case of characters, using the keywords *capitalize* (capital first letter only), *uppercase*, *lowercase* or *none*.

Text layout

text-align

This is identical to the HTML **ALIGN** option, taking the keyword *left*, *right*, *center* and *justify*.

    P {text-align:left}

text-indent

This sets the indent of the first line of a paragraph. The length can be given in *em* (width of the letter 'm'), *cm*, *px* (pixels) or as a percentage of the element's width.

    P {text-indent:2cm}
    P {text-indent:1em}

line-height

This sets the distance between the baselines of text – i.e. between the bottom of the letters in one line and those on the line below. It can be given as:

- the keyword *normal*, setting it to 120% of the font height;
- a *multiple* of the font size; e.g. for 1½ line-spacing:

      P {line-height:1.5}

- a *percentage multiple* of the font size; e.g. for double-spacing:

      P {line-height:200%}

- a *fixed size*, in units of em, cm or px.

When the line height is given as a multiple, the line height in any child elements are multiplied by the same value; in other cases, the resultant height is inherited.

vertical-align

This sets the position of the text in relation to the baseline. There are several keywords of which only *sub* (subscript) and *super* (superscript) have any noticeable effect.

word-spacing

This sets the distance between words, given in ems.

letter-spacing

This sets the distance between letters in a word, given in ems.

```
<HTML>
<HEAD>
<TITLE>Text attributes</TITLE>
<STYLE type=text/css>
    BODY {text-align:center}
    H1 {text-transform:capitalize; text-decoration:underline}
    P {text-align:left; text-indent:2cm;font-size:12pt; line-
height:180%}
</STYLE>
</HEAD>
```

```
<BODY>
<BR>
<H1>The headline should be underlined with initial capitals
</H1>
Everything in the body is centre-aligned.
<P>Unless it has been given a different alignment - text in
the P tag will be left-aligned. It is also indented 2cm, and in
12pt.</P>
</BODY>
</HTML>
```

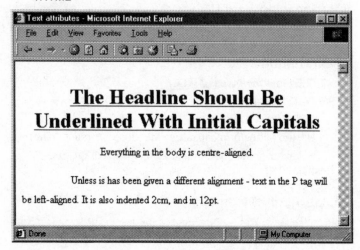

Backgrounds

You can set background colours and images for *any* tag. The same attributes and formats are used.

background-color

This takes a colour name, a hexadecimal value, an **rgb**(*val,val,val*) expression or the keyword *transparent*.

    BODY {background-color:black}

background-image

This takes the expression **URL**(*image_url*) and *image_url* can be the name or a local file or one on the Web.

    BODY {background-image: URL(scenery.gif)}

background-repeat

This defines how the image is shown. *repeat* sets full screen tiling; *repeat-x* duplicates it across the top; *repeat-y* produces a strip down the left; *no-repeat* sets a single image.

    BODY {background-image: URL(logo.gif); background-
    repeat:repeat; background-color:silver}

This tiles the screen with the logo image, or colours the background pale grey if images are not loaded by the browser.

background-attachment

This can be set to *scroll*, so the image moves with the text, or *fixed*, so it stays in place when the page is scrolled.

background-position

This set the horizontal and vertical placing, either by the keywords *top, center, bottom, left, center* or *right*, or by giving the length in cm or px from the top left corner.

```
<HTML>
<HEAD>
<STYLE type=text/css>
  BODY {background-image:URL(stars.gif); background-repeat:repeat}
  H1 {background-image:URL(stripes.gif); color:black; text-align:center}
  P {color:white;font-size:large}
  B {background-color:red; color:white}
</STYLE>
</HEAD>
<BODY>
<BR>
<H1>! Stars and Stripes !</H1>
<P>And other decorative backgrounds can be applied to the whole page, and/or <B>tagged text.</B>
</BODY>
</HTML>
```

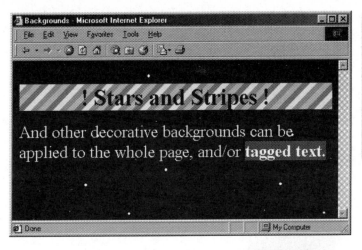

The BODY background uses this small
image, repeated to fill the page

Size of elements

You can control the size and position of all *block elements* – the images, tables, headings, <P> and other tags that create paragraphs.

Values are given in the usual em, cm or px units, or as a percentage of the limits of the parent element.

width and height

These can both be set at a given size, as a percentage of the window or *auto* (the default).

    P {width:80%}

sets the <P> paragraphs to be 80% of the browser width.

    H1 {width:600}

sets Heading 1 to a maximum width of 600 pixels.

Margins and borders

All block elements have margins, borders and padding.

For the BODY element, the box is the edge of the page; for other elements, the box is the padding of the parent element, unless you use the **width** and **height** attributes to set its size.

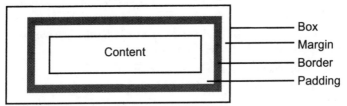

The margin, border and padding all have *width,* which can be anything from 0 upwards. If there is no border, the combined margin and padding values determine the amount of space around the content.

margin

This sets all margins at once. If one size is given, it is applied to all sides. If four are given, they are read as top, right, bottom and left. If there are two or three, the missing values are taken from the opposite side.

You can also set the width of individual margins using **margin-top, margin-right, margin-bottom** and **margin-left**.

padding

This sets all four padding widths at once, as **margin**. For individual settings, use **padding-top**, **padding-right**, **padding-bottom** and **padding-left**.

border-width

This sets all border widths at once, as **margin**. Widths can be given as values or with keywords *thin*, *medium* and *thick*

For individual settings, use **border-top-width**, **border-right-width**, **border-bottom-width**, **border-left-width**.

The simplest approach is to set all four sides the same, e.g.

    P {margin:10%; border-width:5px; padding:0.2cm}

This gives <P> text a margin all round of 10%, a border of 5 pixels, and padding of 0.2cm.

    P {margin: 5% 10%; padding:0.2cm 0.5cm 0.1cm; border-
    width 20}

This sets the margins to the top and bottom at 5%, to the left and right margins at 10%; padding of 0.2cm at the top, 0.5cm to left and right and 0.1cm at the bottom; and a border of 20 pixels all round.

Border colour and style

border-color

This sets the colour of the whole border. Use the colour names or values as for text colour (see page 9).

Sides can be coloured individually by specifying **border-top-color**, **border-left-color**, **border-right-color** and **border-bottom-color**.

border-style

This can be set to *solid*, *double*, *groove*, *ridge*, *inset*, *outset*, *dashed*, *dotted* or *none*. Note that you need widths of 6 pixels or more to see most of these effects.

```
<HTML>
<HEAD>
<TITLE>Margins and borders</TITLE>
<STYLE type=text/css>
    BODY {border-color:lime; border-width:0.5cm;border-
    style:ridge; padding:0.25 cm; text-align:center}
    H1 {border-color:red;border-width:8 16 8 16; border-
        style:inset; color:blue; padding:0.5cm}
    P {margin:.5cm;width:80%;border-width:6px; border-
        style:double; padding:0.5cm}
</STYLE>
</HEAD>
```

```
<BODY>
<H1>Margins and borders</H1>
<P>Borders can add colour to a page, or pick out an item for
special attention.
</BODY>
</HTML>
```

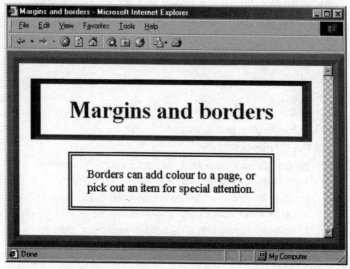

This looks much better in colour! Experiment with different style settings and colours to see how they affect the appearance.

Images and text

There are two additional attributes for image elements.

float

This has the settings *left*, *right* or *none*. It aligns an image to the left or right of the window. Any subsequent text will normally be printed directly after the start of it, with the effect the image 'floats' on top of the text. To stop this, you must set the **clear** attribute.

clear

This determines whether space is needed for text. The settings are:

- *none* says display text beside – or between – floating images.
- *left* and *right* insists there must be clear space to the left (right). The text starts printing on the next line below the floating image.
- *both* holds the display until there are no floating elements on either side.

Classes

A class is a named subset of a tag. Classes allow you to have almost infinite variety on your pages, as you can have any number of styles to the same HTML tag. For example, write these definitions in the **STYLE** block:

H1 {font-size:30pt; color:green}

H1.redhead {font-style:italic; color:red}

H1.bluehead {color:blue}

and you will then have three **<H1>** tag styles. As well as the basic **<H1>** you also have the **redhead** and **bluehead** classes.

Within the **BODY** they are used like this:

<H1>This heading is 30 point in green</H1>

<H1 CLASS = redhead>This is 30 point in red italics</H1>

<H1 CLASS = bluehead>This is 30 point in blue</H1>

All classes of **<H1>** inherit the default settings for the tag and any styles applied to the basic tag, but settings defined for a class override any inherited ones.

ID

A class is an alternative format for a single tag. An ID gives you a format that can be applied to *any* tag – it allows you to set several attribute settings at once, whenever needed.

Define it in the **STYLE** area – note # before the name:

```
#redbox {border-color:red; border-width:10px; padding:5px}
```

Apply as required, using **ID** and the name, but without the #:

```
<H2 ID = redbox>This is important</H2>
```

The next example shows the use of classes and IDs.

```
<HTML>
<HEAD>
<TITLE>Class and ID</TITLE>
<STYLE type=text/css>
    H2.bluehead {font-weight:800;color:blue}
    P {font-size:14pt; font-style:italic}
    P.parared {color:red; font-style:normal}
    p.paraheavy{font-weight:800}
    #boxed {border-width:6; border-style:solid; padding: 5;
border-color:red}
</STYLE>
</HEAD>
```

```
<BODY>
<H2>Class and ID</H2>
<P>Classes allow you to have a greater range of styles
<H2 CLASS= bluehead>Same tag, different effect</H2>
<P CLASS = parared>Classes inherit styles from simple tag
definitions
<H2 ID = boxed>IDs extend</H2>
<P ID = boxed>With an ID you can apply the same formatting
to different tags
<P CLASS = paraheavy ID = boxed> and you can use both at
once
</BODY>
</HTML>
```

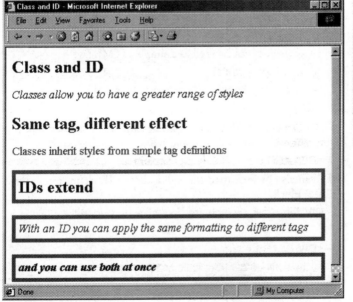

Setting colours is a very visible way to test the effect of class definitions – but only on screen!

<DIV>

<DIV> marks off a division of the page in which a special format can be applied. It can be used as a simple HTML tag:

```
<DIV ALIGN = center>
    ... text and images all centred in here ...
</DIV>
```

<DIV> can take STYLE specifications. This sets up a section in which the text is right-aligned and red.

```
<DIV STYLE = text-align:right;color:red>
```

DIV can also be formatted through a class or ID definition in the STYLE block.

```
DIV.cent {text-align:centre; font-size:16pt; font-style:italic}
...
<DIV CLASS = cent>
    text will be centred, italic in 16 point
</DIV>
```

The same effect could be achieved by using an ID – and the ID style could also be applied to any other suitable tag.

```
#cent {text-align:centre; font-size:16pt; font-style:italic}
...
<DIV ID = cent>
```

<SPAN>

<SPAN> marks off sections *within* blocks of text, e.g.

> Stop when the lights are <SPAN STYLE = color:red>red
> </SPAN> and wait for them to change.

SPAN can be also defined through a class or ID.

> SPAN.loud {font-size:18pt; font-weight:800}
>
>   ...
>
>   This is really <SPAN CLASS = loud>important</SPAN>

The next example demonstrates <DIV> and <SPAN>.

```
<HTML>
<HEAD>
<TITLE>Div and Span</TITLE>
 <STYLE type=text/css>
  P {font-size:18pt; font-face:arial}
  SPAN.initial {font-size:30pt; font-face:serif; color:black}
  DIV.standout {color:green; font-style:italic; border-width:10;
    border-style:ridge}
 </STYLE>
</HEAD>
<BODY>
<H1>The Spider's Web</H1>
<DIV STYLE = color:red>
```

```
    <P><SPAN class=initial>O</SPAN>nce upon a time there
was a <SPAN STYLE = font-size:10pt>very small</SPAN>
Web ...</P>
</DIV>
```

This tale of how a little spider called Hotmetal span a web and span it some more until it covered the whole world, is available now from all good bookstores

```
<P>
<DIV CLASS=standout ALIGN = center>
  or direct from <SPAN class=initial>C</SPAN>ern <SPAN
class=initial> S</SPAN>tory <SPAN class=initial>S</
SPAN>tore
</DIV>
</BODY>
</HTML>
```

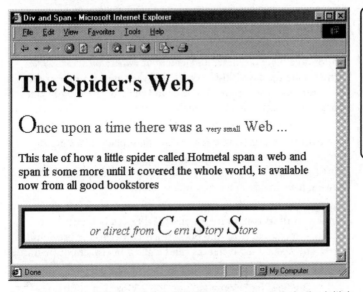

One of the most obvious uses of SPAN in this example is in the initial class that creates the large initial letters.

Layers

The basic idea behind layers is simple – by adding position information to a tag, you locate an element anywhere on screen. The elements are displayed in the order that they appear in the code, with later ones overlapping earlier – in layers. In theory, you can set a position on any tag, but it only really works with <DIV>. This is not a big problem – you just put <DIV> around the element.

The hard work is getting things in the right place! Planning the layout helps, but trial and error gets you there in the end. (And don't forget that if the page is going onto the Web, people will be viewing it in a wide range of window sizes.)

position can be set *absolute* – measured from the top left of the window or of its containing element (**DIV**s can be nested) – or *relative* – measured from the bottom left corner of the previous layer. The *top* and *left* distances can be given in em, cm or px units.

You can define the layer as a class in the **STYLE** area:

        DIV.flow {position:absolute; top:200px; left:300px}

or directly within the <DIV> tag

    <DIV STYLE=position:absolute; top:100px; left:100px>

An example will help. Experiment with the values and order to see the effect. Change the order in which they are written in the code to change the layering order.

```
<HTML>
<HEAD>
<STYLE type=text/css>
    H1 {text-align:center; border-width:6px; border-style:ridge;
border-color:blue; background-color:lime}

    B {font-weight:800; font-size:14pt; color:red}

    P {border-width:5px; border-style:solid; padding:10px;
border-color:red; background-color:yellow}

    DIV.pic {position:absolute; top:20px; left:50px}

    DIV.eggtext {position:absolute; top:275px; left:225px}
</STYLE>
</HEAD>
<BODY>
<H1>Layers</H1>
<DIV CLASS = pic> <IMG SRC = chicken.gif> </DIV>
<DIV STYLE="position:absolute; top:150px; left:100px">
    <P>Which came first? The chicken... </DIV>
<DIV STYLE="position:absolute; top:180px; left:300px">
    <IMG SRC = egg.gif> </DIV>
<DIV CLASS = eggtext>
    <P> ... or the egg</P> </DIV>
</BODY>
</HTML>
```

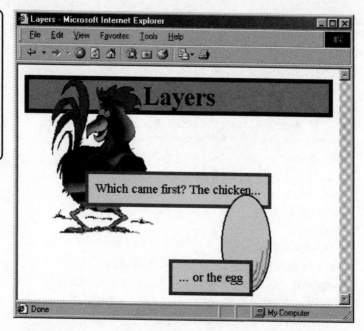

Overlapping makes the use of layers very visible, but the real point is that you can place elements exactly where you want them. Notice that positions can be defined in the STYLE block or in the DIV tag – use whichever gives more readable code.

External style sheets

One big advantage of style sheets is that they make it much simpler
to create and maintain consistency across a site. The site's designer
can set up free standing style sheets, containing nothing but
definitions, which can be linked into pages to set styles. The linking
lines look like this:

```
<LINK REL=STYLESHEET TYPE=text/css HREF=corp.css>
```

There might just be one sheet for the whole site, or one sheet to set
the overall corporate design, then a number of second level ones for
departments – and perhaps third or fourth level ones too. The lower
level sheets will normally be there to adjust the basic design, not
replace it. The design can be tweaked further by **STYLE** settings
within the pages.

The **<LINK>** and **<STYLE>** tags must be written in cascading
order. Settings are applied as the code is processed, so that later
settings override earlier ones.

Creating a style sheet

Definitions of tags, classes and IDs are written in the same way as in
a **STYLE** area, though without the **<STYLE>** tags. A style sheet file
could redefine a whole range of tags, and have classes for every
occasion, or it might just define one or two aspects. The main
advantage is that it can control the appearance of many pages, and
redefining that one file will reformat every page that is linked to it.

Comments to identify the sheet or explain formats can be added as required, but should be written inside /* … */ markers. The file is saved as text, with a **.css** extension.

Here's the first sheet, which sets the corporate styles.

```
/* corporate style sheet */
    BODY {background-color:yellow}
    P {font-size:14pt; margin-left:10px; margin-right:20px}
    H1, H2, H3, H4 {font-family:tahoma,arial,sans-serif; text-
        align:center}
    ADDRESS {background-color:red;padding:5px; border-
        width:5px; border-style:groove; border-color:blue}
```

The next sheet gives the department's variations, which simply change some colours, leaving all the size and layout formatting untouched.

```
/* departmental style sheet for Sales */
    P {color:maroon}
    H1, H2, H3, H4 {color:navy}
    ADDRESS {border-color:navy}
```

The page code links in the two sheets, then redefines some text tags.

```
<HTML>
<HEAD>
 <TITLE>External style sheets</TITLE>
<!The two external sheets are linked>
```

```
  <LINK REL=STYLESHEET TYPE=text/css HREF=corp.css>
  <LINK REL=STYLESHEET TYPE=text/css HREF=sales.css>
<!Then the special styles for the page are defined>
  <STYLE TYPE = text/css>
    H1, H2 {border-width:4; border-style:solid; background-
      color:white}
    P {font-weight:bold; background-color:lime}
    ADDRESS {text-align:center}
    </STYLE>
  </HEAD>


  <BODY>
    <H1>Colossal Summer Savings!</H1>
    <H2>Special Offers</H2>
    <H3>Domain Names</H3>
    <P>Buy One Get One Free! Choose from .TV, .CO, .IT and
      .IN
    <H3>Web site design</H3>
    <P>From concept to completion, full service, satisfaction
      guaranteed. <BR>
    Start July or August to get a 20% discount and be ready
      for Xmas</P>
<ADDRESS>E-mail your order to
```

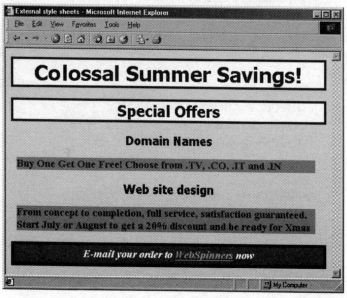

```
<A HREF = mailto: sales@webs.con> WebSpinners</A> now
</ADDRESS>
</BODY>
</HTML>
```

Compare the resulting display with the two style sheet files and the
HTML code to see which features are set at which stage. What
would be the effect of linking the sheet files in a different order?

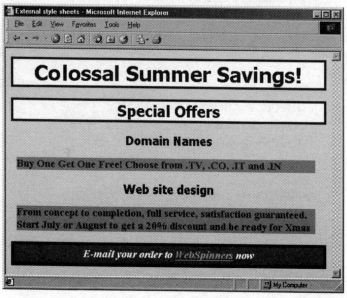

10

publishing your pages

Preparation

When your page and image files are uploaded to your ISP's server, they will normally all be stored in one folder. (You may be able to create subfolders within your part of their system, but that creates complexities you do not need.) Set up a new folder on your own system and copy into it the files that make up your home page set. Having everything in one place – a place that is not cluttered up with unwanted files – will make life easier when you upload.

Final test

Run your browser, turn off the image loading and open your home page file.

- How does it look as a text-only page?
- If you have several linked pages, use the links to check out each one. Can you move between all the pages?
- Do the page all look OK in text-only mode?

Work through the pages again, downloading the images as you go.

- Are all the images displayed correctly?
- Are you happy with the layout?

If you have any design changes to make, now is the time to do it. (Though you can edit and upload new versions of your pages – or add more, delete or replace the lot – at any point in the future.)

Your service provider

Before you can upload to your service provider, you need to know where to put your files, how to get them there, and what to call your home page – the top one of the set – when it is on site.

At most Internet service providers the home page must be called *index.html* (note the 'L' at the end – see the Tip below). The fact that every user's home page has the same name is irrelevant, as each is in its own folder, and will be identified by its path. Exactly where your files will be stored is generally irrelevant. They will normally be somewhere on an FTP server, and when you log in to that server, it will take you directly to your directory.

Read their documentation and their on-line help (if any) and if that still doesn't tell you what you need to know, ring up and ask.

On the Unix systems that most ISPs use, HTML documents are identified by the extension .HTML. On a PC, they normally have the extension .HTM, though Windows permits the use of .HTML. Your ISP, like my local one at TCP, may insist that the home page document has an .HTML name, though subsidiary pages can have the .HTM extension. If this is the case, go through your pages now and edit any links back to the home page to add 'L' to the end of the name. If necessary, you can change the home page's name after you have uploaded it.

WS_FTP

This is the standard Windows application for handling your end of an FTP connection. If you do not have a copy, get one now. You can download it through your browser from the home site of its author (John Junod), at:

www.ipswitch.com

The FTP connection

If you have used FTP before, it will probably have been to connect to one of the public FTP sites. With these, you log in as Anonymous, giving your e-mail name as a password. (WS_FTP will have collected this from you during installation, so you won't need to enter it for each new site.) Once at an FTP site you have limited access – downloading from public directories and uploading to designated incoming ones. You cannot normally create directories or rename or delete files. Logging in to your own directory on your provider's system is a different matter, as this is *your* place. You – and only you – have control here.

tip

On Web servers, folders are called directories. In fact, this is what they were called on all computers before Microsoft decided that folders sounded better.

Accessing your Web space

Log in to your service, then run WS_FTP. It should start with the Session Profile panel open. If it is not open, click on the **Connect** button to open it.

Click New, then type in a **Profile name** for the connection – this can be anything that is meaningful to you.

For the **Host name**, enter the name of your provider's FTP server. The **User ID** and **Password** are the same as the ones that you use to get online with your browser. If no one else has access to your PC, tick **Save Pwd** so that you don't need to enter it in future.

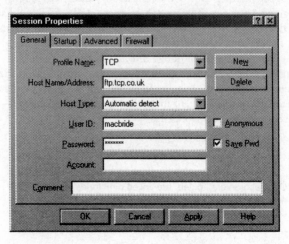

You can change directory after you have logged in, but it is quicker and simpler to do it now. Switch to the **Startup** tab. If you have been given the path to your directory at the service provider, enter it into the **Initial Remote Host Directory** slot. (Don't worry if you haven't been told – it almost certainly means you don't need to know.) Enter the path to the home page files' directory in the **Initial Local Directory** slot.

```
Session Properties                                    ? X

 General  Startup  Advanced  Firewall

   Initial Remote Host Directory:
   /m/macbride

   Initial Local Directory:
   C:\homepage

   Initialize Command: [use ';' to separate multiple commands]


   Local file mask:            Time offset in hours:   0

   Remote file mask:


              OK        Cancel        Apply        Help
```

Click **OK** to move to the main screen. You are ready to upload.

Uploading

If everything is set up correctly, you should see a succession of messages scrolling through the narrow bottom pane of the WS_FTP window. Though some may be cryptic, and others move off before you have had a chance to read them, you should see enough to know that the connection is being made. You will know that you are

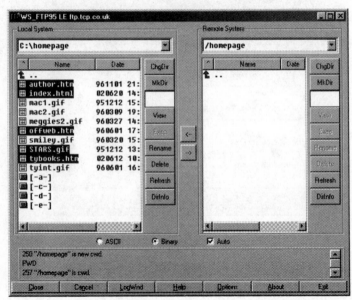

there and ready to upload when you see your directory's name displayed at the *Remote System* slot at the top right of the window, and other activity ceases.

Select the files in your home page directory, and click ⟶ to send them to the remote system.

With larger files, you will see a Transfer Status panel open, displaying the progress of the uploading. HTML files are normally so small and transfer so quickly that all you see is a flash on the screen.

The whole set shouldn't take more than a few minutes to upload. After the last one has gone in, the directory listing on the Remote System pane will update. Check that they are all there, and if they are, click **Close** to shut down the FTP connection and click **Exit** to close WS_FTP.

Web Publishing Wizard

Windows users can upload their files with Web Publishing Wizard. There are several ways to use this. Here is the simplest way.

Locate all the files that you want to upload, and place them in a folder by themselves – if necessary make a new folder to hold them.

Contact your Internet Service Provider and find the URL of your Web space – this may be either an http:// or an ftp:// URL.

1 Start the Wizard. The first job is to select the folder – click **Browse Folders** and locate your home page folder.

2   Give the server a name – any name will do as long as it means
    something to you.

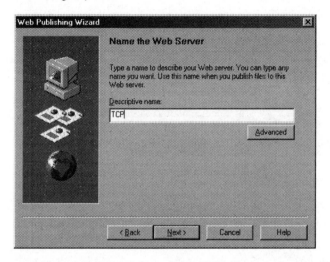

3   Enter the URL for your home page. The path to the local
    directory will have been copied in from the first stage of the
    Wizard. Notice that in the URL, a forward slash is used to
    separate the different parts of the address, but in the path to the
    local directory, you use a backslash.

4   At the next stage, click **Finish** to start uploading the pages. The
    Wizard will start up your dial-up connection, if necessary, then

post the files, one by one, up to the server. Uploading is slower through the Web than using FTP, but it still shouldn't take long.

Web Publishing Wizard

Specify the URL and Directory

Type the URL or Internet address you use to access your personal Web pages (for example, http://www.microsoft.com/myname). Your system administrator or service provider supplies this address.

URL or Internet address:

http://homepages.tcp.co.uk/~macbride

Type the local directory on your computer that will correspond to the URL entered above.

Local directory:

C:\homepage\

< Back   Next >   Cancel   Help

tip

The first time that you use the Wizard, you will probably want to upload the whole set that makes up your home page system. Later, you will normally only be uploading any new and edited files. Moving these into a separate folder will make uploading easier – you can simply send the whole folder.

Testing

Your home page should be accessible from the Web within a few minutes of uploading your files. If you haven't already found out your URL – you would have needed it if you had used the Web Publishing Wizard – go to your service provider's site, or ring them, now and find out.

Run your browser, get on-line and use the **File > Open** command to go to your home page. Can you get there? If not, it may be that their system is a little slow on recognizing the presence of new home page files.

Does it look as good on-line as it did during testing? Do the images download at a reasonable speed? Do the links all work? Remember that now you can test the links to other people's pages, FTP files, etc., as well as the links between your own pages.

Is it back to the drawing board, or is it time to let other people know that you are there?

Publicity for your page

The key question here is 'Who do you want to visit you?'

If the aim is to make this a place for family and friends to drop in to pick up your latest news, then the best way to publicize your page is to ring them up and tell them that it's there.

If you have assembled links and information about your hobby or special interest, and would like to share this with fellow enthusiasts, then post an article in the relevant newsgroups announcing your arrival on the scene (and hit the directories – see below).

If yours is a business home page, there may still be relevant newsgroups where an announcement would be welcomed, but this must be done thoughtfully. Some groups are distinctly non-commercial and do not appreciate business advertising – an announcement there could produce a flood of complaints in your e-mail. Some groups accept – and some are designed for – business home page announcements. Don't post to groups you don't know. Join and read enough of the articles in a newsgroup to get its flavour before you post to it.

If you are running an enthusiasts' resource page or a business page, or if you are a plain old-fashioned extrovert, *hit the directories*. There are several hundred directories on the Internet – large and small, specialized and general. Get your page into some or all of those and you should have visitors.

You can submit your page's URL to individual directories. The best way to do this is to go to the directory and look for a *Submit* sign. If you don't see one, they probably don't take unsolicited links. Amongst others, you might like to try:

Yahoo (www.yahoo.com),

Excite (www.excite.com/directory)

Lycos (http://www.lycos.co.uk/service/addasite.html)

The second approach is to use a site promotion service such as AddMe (www.addme.com). They will take your URL and details of your pages and submit them to the Web directories and search engines. AddMe offer a free service, which will get you into Lycos, Google, Excite and a dozen or so other major sites. They also offer a professional service which will promote your site much more widely and give you analysis and feedback.

Counters

A counter will tell you how many people have visited your page. Now, you cannot actually count them yourself, but there are Web organizations that can do it for you. Their services are usually free – it is something they do to advertise their Web presence.

I got my counter from Net Digits, at:

> http://www.digits.com

Contact them when you have got your home page up and running successfully. There is a form to fill in, to give them the details of your page, and to set up your counter at their site. Once it has been created, you can write a link to it into your home page.

The link is written into an <IMG SRC ...> tag, and should look something like this:

> <IMG SRC = "http://counter.digits.com/wc/maccount">

Obviously, the URL will depend upon the counter service you use and the name you choose.

The counter can be embedded in some text:

> You are visitor no. <IMG SRC = "http://counter.digits.com/wc/maccount"> since 21st October 2001

Other organizations offering free counters include, GoStats at:

> http://gostats.com/counter.html

and Microsoft's bCentral at:

> http://www.bcentral.com

11 appendices

HTML tags and options

Structure

<HTML> </HTML> Enclose the whole document

<HEAD> </HEAD> Enclose the information area

<TITLE></TITLE> Define the name to appear in the title bar, and in browsers' Favorites.

<META> Used to carry the author's name, search keywords and other information.

> **NAME** = *Author* – name of page's author;
>
>> *Keywords* – comma separated list of words or "phrases in quotes" for use by search engines;
>>
>> *Categories* – list of words or "phrases" for use by Web directories.
>
> **LANG** specifies the language using standard abreviations, e.g. en = English, fr = French, sp = Spanish.

<ISINDEX> Defines phrases for keyword searches.

<BASE HREF = ...> Sets the base URL. Use it where files are stored in a set of folders and subfolders.

<SCRIPT> Defines the scripting language, e.g. JavaScript, that is used on the page.

<APPLET ...> Defines a Java applet.

<STYLE TYPE = text/css> ... </STYLE> to enclose a style definition block in an HTML document.

...TYPE = text/css STYLE = *style definitions* ... can be used within most tags to define a style within the BODY.

<LINK REL=STYLESHEET TYPE=text/css HREF = url> to create a link to a .css style sheet file.

<BODY> </BODY> Enclose the displayed page.

> **BACKGROUND = *Image*,** repeated if space available
>
> **BGCOLOR = *Colour value*** of background
>
> **TEXT = *Colour value*** of text
>
> **LINK = *Colour value*** of unvisited links
>
> **VLINK = *Colour value*** of visited links
>
> **ALINK = *Colour value*** of active links.

<DIV ...> ... </DIV> encloses a set of elements within a page for styling. Styles can be defined directly within the <DIV> tag, or indirectly through a CLASS or ID option.

> **CLASS = *classname*** used within a tag to select a class definition for that tag.
>
> **ID = *idname*** also used within a tag to select a named definition for that tag.

<SPAN> ... </SPAN> as <DIV>, but enclosing an area within an element.

<!... *comment* ...> Not displayed by browser

Headings and breaks

\<H*n*>\</H*n*> Heading at level *n*: 1 is largest, 6 the smallest

\<P> Start of Paragraph

   ALIGN = *Left/Center/Right* aligns text

**\
** Line Break

\<HR> Horizontal Rule

   SIZE = *Value* in pixels

   WIDTH = *Value* in pixels or percentage

   NOSHADE Makes the line solid

\<PRE>\</PRE> Preformatted text; preserves line breaks

\<ADDRESS>\</ADDRESS> Normally holds author's address

\<CENTER>\</CENTER> Centres text (or images)

Character formats

\<B>\</B> Bold

\<BIG> set to 'large' font size as defined by the browser.

\<BLOCKQUOTE> displays text indented from both margins.

\<CITE>\</CITE> Citation – used for quotations

\<CODE>\</CODE> Computer source code

\<EM>\</EM> Emphasized = \<I>

\<FONT ...>\</FONT> Enclosed text to be formatted with one or more of these options:

    SIZE = *Number*, 1 to 7 (largest) for size of text

    COLOR = *Colour value* of following text

    FACE = *Font name* or family

<I></I> *Italic*

<KBD></KBD> Keyboard entry = **<TT>**

<S> *or* **<STRIKE>** strikethrough

<SAMP></SAMP> Text sample

<SMALL> set to 'small' font size as defined by the browser

<STRONG></STRONG> Strongly emphasized = **<B>**

**** Superscript

**** Subscript

<TT></TT> `Typewriter`

<VAR></VAR> Variable names, displayed in italics

Lists

<UL></UL> Unordered (bulleted) List

    TYPE = *disc/circle/square*

    COMPACT if set, reduces the spaces between lines

<OL></OL> Ordered (numbered or lettered) List

    TYPE = 1 (numbers), a (lower case letters), A (capital letters),

    i (lower case roman numerals), I (capital roman numerals)

START = first number in the sequence

COMPACT reduces the spacing between items

<LI> List Item

<DL></DL> Definition List

<DT> Term in definition list

<DD> Definition

Images

<IMG SRC = *Image*> Displays the *Image* (GIF or JPG)

   ALT = *Text* to display if image is not downloaded

   ALIGN = *Top/Bottom/Middle* aligns following text

   HEIGHT = *Value* in pixels or percentage of window height

   WIDTH = *Value* in pixels or percentage of window width

   BORDER = *Value* in pixels

   HSPACE = **VSPACE** = *Value* in pixels to create space around the image

   USEMAP = *Name* identifies the image for use with MAP

<MAP NAME = ...> links to the image named by **USEMAP**

<AREA > defines a hyperlink in an image map

   HREF= *url* the linked **PAGE**

   TARGET = the frame or window in which to load the page

ALT = text displayed when the mouse pauses over the image or if the image is not loaded

SHAPE = *rect/circ/poly*

COORDS = co-ordinates of the top left and bottom right corners of a rectangle; or the centre point and radius of a circle; or of all the vertices of a polygon, repeating the first at the end.

Links and anchors

<A HREF = *URL>Link*</A> Hypertext link between *Link* text or image and local or remote *URL*

<A NAME = *Target> Text*</A> Creates a jump target in a page

Forms

<FORM...></FORM> Encloses the Form area

METHOD = *Post* (*Get*, not covered here, also possible)

ACTION = Your e-mail address

<INPUT ...> Data entry by visitor

NAME = *Name* of variable to store data

SIZE = *Width* in characters

TYPE = *Checkbox/Radio* options

Reset/Submit buttons

Password hides input text

> *Hidden* does not appear in the display
>
> *Image* creates a clickable image
>
> *Button* creates a 'blank' button

VALUE = *Value* returned in feedback

CHECKED if set, the checkbox.radio is selected at the start

<TEXTAREA ...> Multi-line text entry

NAME = *Name* of variable to store data

ROWS = *Number* of rows to display

COLS = *Number* of columns to display

<SELECT ...> Sets up a drop-down list

NAME = *Name* of variable to store data

SIZE = *Number* of items to display at one time

MULTIPLE Allow multiple selections

<OPTION VALUE = *RetVal> ListItem* Display *ListItem* in Select list; pass *RetVal* to NAME variable

</SELECT> Closes Select list

Tables

<TABLE ...></TABLE> Encloses Table code

ALIGN = *Left/Right/Center*

BACKGROUND = *Width* of border; narrow if no *width* given;

BGCOLOR = *Colour name* or *value*

BORDER = *Width* of border; narrow if no *width* given;

CELLSPACING = *Value* in pixels of distance between inner and outer borders

CELLPADDING = *Value* in pixels of distance between inner border and text or image

WIDTH = *Value* in pixels or percentage

<CAPTION ...></CAPTION> Encloses text of caption

ALIGN = *Top/Bottom* – default to *Top*

<TR></TR> Encloses a row

<TH ...></TH> Enclose a row or column header cell

<TD ...></TD> Enclose a data cell

COLSPAN = *Number* of columns to spread cell across

ROWSPAN = *Number* of rows to stretch cell down

ALIGN = *Left/Right/Center* horizontal alignment of item in header or data cell

VALIGN = *Top/Middle/Bottom* vertical alignment

WIDTH = *Value* in pixels for width of cell

<COLGROUP > defines a group of columns in a table.

SPAN is the number of columns

WIDTH the size, in pixels, of each.

<COL> marks each column in a group

    SPAN sets how many columns are spanned by the current one
    SPAN=0 means *all* remaining columns in the group

    WIDTH sets the size in pixels

<THEAD> header information in a table, enables more efficient printing and database analysis

<TFOOT> provides footer information

<TBODY> contains the code for the main table

Frames

<FRAMESET ...> Start of frame section, in layout document and replacing the normal BODY elements. The tag must contain either a ROWS or COLS option.

    ROWS = Divides the window into frames horizontally, specifying the size of each either in pixels, or as a percentage of the space, or using '*' to share remaining space.

    COLS = Divides the window into frames vertically, specifying sizes as above

</FRAMESET> End of frame section

<FRAME ...> Defines the content and nature of a frame

    SRC = URL of document

    NAME = Name of frame, if to be used as TARGET of HREF link

SCROLLING = *Yes/No/Auto* – controls appearance of scroll bars around frame

NORESIZE Forces fixed size frame

<NOFRAMES></NOFRAMES> Encloses code to be displayed in browsers which cannot handle frames

TARGET = *Name/Self/Parent/Top/Blank* – HREF option to specify where a document is to be displayed

Style sheets summary

Keywords used for settings are shown in *italics*.

Sizes can be given in units of em, cm or px (pixels).

Colours can be given as names or by *rgb(red_val, green_val, blue_val)* where values are numbers in the range 0 to 255.

none setting is used to turn off settings turned on elsewhere.

Font

font-family: font names (in "quotes" if they contain spaces) with a generic name as last alternative. The generic names are *serif, sans-serif, cursive, fantasy, monospace*.

font-style: *normal, italic* or *oblique*

font-variant: *normal* or *small-caps*

font-weight: *lighter, normal, bold, bolder* or a value 100, 200 … 900

font-size: *xx-small, x-small, small, medium, large, x-large, xx-large, larger, smaller*, a percentage or size in points (*pt*)

font: list of values for all or some of font-style, font-variant, font-weight, font-size and font-family

color: colour_value

Background

background-color: colour_value or *transparent*

background-image: *url* (hyperlink or filename) or *none*

background-repeat: *repeat, repeat-x, repeat-y* or *no-repeat*

background-attachment: *scroll* or *fixed*

background-position: distance from top and left as percentage or size; or keywords *top, center* or *bottom, left, center* or *right*

background: list of values for background-color; background-image; background-repeat; background-attachment; background-position

Text properties

word-spacing: *normal* or value in ems

letter-spacing: *normal* or value in ems

text-align: *left, right, center* or *justify*

vertical-align: *baseline, sub, super, text-top, middle, text-bottom*, sets alignment relative to the parent element – could be used to pick out a word in a paragraph

text-indent: *value* in ems, cm or px, or as a percentage of the window

line-height: *normal* or size, or as a percentage of the font size – sets the distance between lines of text in a paragraph

text-decoration: *none, underline, overline, line-through* or *blink*

text-transform: *capitalize* (initial), *uppercase, lowercase, none* (used to cancel setting inherited from parent element or style sheet)

Box properties

These control the size, position and borders of elements.

width: size, percentage of window or *auto*.

height: size, percentage of window or *auto*

float: *left*, *right* or *none*

clear: *none*, *left*, *right* or *both*

margin: sets all the margins at once. If one size is given, it is applied to all sides. If four are given, they are read as top, right, bottom and left. If there are two or three, the missing values are taken from the opposite side.

margin-top, margin-right, margin-bottom, margin-left: size, percentage of window or *auto* – sets each margin separately

padding: sets all four at once, as **margin**

padding-top, padding-right, padding-bottom, padding-left: size, or percentage of window – sets each padding separately

border-width: sets all border widths at once. As margin except that if two sizes are given, top and bottom widths are set to the first, right and left are set to the second.

border-top-width, border-right-width, border-bottom-width, border-left-width: *thin*, *medium*, *thick* or size – sets each width separately

border-color: from one to four colour names or values, applied to the sides as for **border-width**

border-style: one to four of *none, dotted, dashed, solid, double, groove, ridge, inset, outset,* applied to the sides as for **border-width** above

border: up to three values to set border-width, border-style and color for all four sides at once

Lists

list-style-type: *disc, circle, square, decimal, lower-roman, upper-roman, lower-alpha, upper-alpha* or *none* – combines the UL and OL TYPE options for the <LI> tag

list-style-image: *url(hyperlink or filename)* or *none* – sets an image as the bullet for a list item

list-style-position: *inside* or *outside* – sets the position of the bullet in relation to the list item

Miscellaneous

display: *block, inline, list-item* or *none* (turns off the display of the element)

Elements fall naturally into three categories: block, e.g. P, H1 and IMG; inline, e.g. B and I; and list-item, LI. They can be redefined into another category – though you would need a convincing reason to mess with this!

white-space: *normal, pre* (as <PRE> tag) or *nowrap*

A:link, A:visited, A:active *colour_value* set colours for links

Hexadecimal

People naturally work in base 10 because they have 10 fingers. Computers naturally work with binary (base 2) numbers, because they have two electronic 'fingers' – on and off. Binary numbers are not nice to handle. (Read these aloud: 01001011 and 01011010.)

Hexadecimal (base 16) is a compromise. The numbers are easily converted into binary (16 = 2 × 2 × 2 × 2) and easy for people to read. Hexadecimal uses 16 'fingers', so the digits '0' to '9' are not enough. The letters 'A' to 'F' are pressed into service.

Base 10	Hex		Base 10	Hex	
0	0		17	11	
1	1		18	12	
2	2		19	13	
3	3		20	14	
4	4		21	15	
5	5		22	16	
6	6		23	17	
7	7		24	18	
8	8		25	19	
9	9		26	1A	
10	A		27	1B	
11	B		28	1C	
12	C		29	1D	
13	D		30	1E	
14	E		31	1F	
15	F		32	20	
16	10 (a 'handful')		33	21	etc.

Hexadecimal numbers are usually written as a pair of digits. To work out their base 10 value, multiply the first by 16 and add the second. For example:

2B	= 2 × 16 + 11(B)	= 43
80	= 8 × 16 + 0	= 128
FF	= 15(F) × 16 + 15	= 255

FF is the biggest number you can write with 2 digits. It is also the biggest value that can be held in 1 byte.

Character codes

As HTML pages are plain text files, characters outside the standard ASCII set are not recognized. A few characters, such as '<' and '>' have special meaning to HTML, and so cannot be simply written as normal text. To display any of these in your pages, use these character codes giving either the name or the number, with an ampersand before and semi-colon after, e.g. **À** or À.

Accented letters

Agrave	#192	À	Ntilde	#209	Ñ
Aacute	#193	Á	Ograve	#210	Ò
Acirc	#194	Â	Oacute	#211	Ó
Atilde	#195	Ã	Ocirc	#212	Ô
Auml	#196	Ä	Otilde	#213	Õ
Aring	#197	Å	Ouml	#214	Ö
AElig	#198	Æ	Oslash	#216	Ø
Ccedil	#199	Ç	Ugrave	#217	Ù
Egrave	#200	È	Uacute	#218	Ú
Eacute	#201	É	Ucirc	#219	Û
Ecirc	#202	Ê	Uuml	#220	Ü
Euml	#203	Ë	Yacute	#221	Ý
Igrave	#204	Ì	szlig	#223	ß
Iacute	#205	Í	agrave	#224	à
Icirc	#206	Î	aacute	#225	á
Iuml	#207	Ï	acirc	#226	â

atilde	#227	ã		ntilde	#241	ñ
auml	#228	ä		ograve	#242	ò
aring	#229	å		oacute	#243	ó
aelig	#230	æ		ocirc	#244	ô
ccedil	#231	ç		otilde	#245	õ
egrave	#232	è		ouml	#246	ö
eacute	#233	é		oslash	#248	ø
ecirc	#234	ê		ugrave	#249	ù
euml	#235	ë		uacute	#250	ú
igrave	#236	ì		ucirc	#251	û
iacute	#237	í		uuml	#252	ü
icirc	#238	î		yacute	#253	ý
iuml	#239	ï		yuml	#255	ÿ

Currency and other symbols

iexcl	#161	¡		frac14	#188	¼
cent	#162	¢		frac12	#189	½
pound	#163	£		frac34	#190	¾
curren	#164	¤		iquest	#191	¿
yen	#165	¥		times	#215	×
brvbar	#166	¦		divide	#247	÷
copy	#169	©		quot	#34	"
reg	#174	®		amp	#38	&
deg	#176	°		lt	#60	<
plusmn	#177	±		gt	#62	>
micro	#181	µ				

Useful Web sites

The HTML Working Group
   http://www.w3.org/MarkUp
HTML Writers Guild
   http://www.hwg.org/
AddMe
   http://www.addme.com
Babel (Glossary of Internet acronyms and abbreviations)
   http://www.geocities.com/ikind_babel/babel/babel.html
Google search engine
   http://www.google.com
Java Boutique
   http://javaboutique.internet.com/
The JavaScript Source
   http://javascript.internet.com/
MapEdit
   http://www.boutell.com/index.html
Microsoft Developer Network
   http://msdn.microsoft.com/library
Shareware Central
   http://www.shareware.com